The Language of Success

The Language of Success

*The Confidence and Ability to Say
What You Mean and Mean What
You Say in Business and Life*

Kim Wilkerson and Alan Weiss

BEP BUSINESS EXPERT PRESS

The Language of Success: The Confidence and Ability to Say What You Mean and Mean What You Say in Business and Life

First published in 2016 by
Business Expert Press, LLC
222 East 46th Street, New York, NY 10017
www.businessexpertpress.com

ISBN-13: 978-1-63157-300-2 (paperback)
ISBN-13: 978-1-63157-301-9 (e-book)

Business Expert Press Corporate Communication Collection

Collection ISSN: 2156-8162 (print)
Collection ISSN: 2156-8170 (electronic)

Cover and interior design by Exeter Premedia Services Private Ltd., Chennai, India

First edition: 2016

10 9 8 7 6 5 4 3 2 1

Printed in the United States of America.

To the truly outstanding teachers, mentors, and coaches everywhere, who selflessly help people to discover and apply vast, untapped talents.

Abstract

The Language of Success provides pragmatic and practical advice on how to harness the power of language in business and in life. Influencing for results, creating a culture of intelligent inquiry, utilizing critical questioning skills, and managing critical situations are all integral to success in any setting. In business, this book is essential for leaders and executives. In addition, it is also written for all levels in an organization: senior leaders, directors, managers, supervisors, and individual contributors in any business. This includes large and small, public, private, and not-for-profit organizations, as well as family-owned businesses, boutique firms, and solo entrepreneurs. The concepts, skills, and techniques to achieve results are applicable whether in the office or with family or friends.

In this day and age of intense focus on engagement, commitment, and most significantly, results achieved, the readers will benefit by learning thought-provoking key principles, applicable practices, and techniques to leverage and ensure success with the language they use every day.

Keywords

communications, debate, decision making, executive, influence, intelligent inquiry, leader, leadership, manager, negotiations, objections, persuasion, problem solving, questions, resolving conflict, sales, success

Contents

Acknowledgments

To my mentor, who planted the seed that I should write this book. To my coach, who insisted the time was right for this book. To my coauthor, who was willing, receptive, and instrumental in collaborating on this book. As my mentor, my coach, and my coauthor, thank you, Alan. Your wisdom, influence, and friendship are priceless.

To Pete, Rosie, and Paul ... three people in my life who set the stage for me at a very early age. More than you'll ever know.

—Kim Wilkerson

To all my grammar school teachers who insisted I invest in language skills, which created a better ROI than even Apple stock.

—Alan Weiss

Introduction

The limits of my language mean the limits of my world.

—Ludwig Wittgenstein

"Meow" means "woof" in cat.

—George Carlin

It's always dangerous to write a book about language. Should we have said *work* instead of *book*, or, perhaps, *tome*? Is it actually *dangerous* or merely *fretful*? This kind of self-editing and search for perfection can undermine excellence, and even completion.

Thus, we're after success, not perfection.

Our intent is to provide you with questions, phrasing, responses, and linguistic arabesques that will accelerate your speed, influence others, and gain your objectives. We sometimes consider these approaches the *martial arts of language*. We don't mean to be slick or overpowering, just smart enough to use the existing momentum in our favor, even against much larger opponents and interests.

The heart of powerful language is clarity, and we have a huge arsenal of words to potentially apply. But like Michelangelo, who supposedly claimed that he carved the *David* by taking away everything that didn't resemble David, our goal is to reduce, to cull, to simplify. The true power of language is to use it sparingly and cleanly, a rapier not a bludgeon.

If you use the techniques that follow, you'll find that your personal influence and professional success will grow exponentially. We can't guarantee that because we don't control your discipline and focus. But we trust you will apply discipline and focus as you find the techniques in the book immediately applicable and highly pragmatic.

We hope we've made it clear, short, simple, and useful. That's our language for success.

—Kim Wilkerson, Cedar Rapids, IA
—Alan Weiss, East Greenwich, RI

CHAPTER 1

Our Hesitancy to Question

Why we always say later, "What I should have said ... "
We tend not to question, because we are convinced the other party is an expert,
or the questioning is impolite, or we'll be seen as dolts. These various fears and
myths disempower us from finding truth and acting on it.

Authority Figures and God: Yes, Doctor!

The historical, stereotypical fears include public speaking, flying, heights, and first dates. We've found that you can add to that the fear of questioning authority figures. We act as if our teacher were Aristotle, our guide Odysseus, our stock broker Warren Buffet, and our doctor Louis Pasteur.

We've observed underlings in executive meetings at Fortune 500 companies actually address the CEO as Mr. President, and employees in the hall move out of the way of senior managers bearing down on them as if they were the chambermaids in a Four Seasons Hotel trained to get out of the way of guests.

We tend to imbue people with more than respect, but with an infallibility that would make a pope blush. In our work with hospitals all over the world, the abject refusal of nurses (and even lesser doctors) has resulted in botched operations, prolonged illnesses, and even death. ("Surgeries on wrong limbs" on Google brings up over 830,000 items.) We have a colleague, a former surgeon, Vickie Rackner, who has built a consulting practice on the basis of helping patients gain the courage to ask their doctors the right questions, whether in the hospital or in the office. What is the *right* question?

It's any question that's on your mind related to your condition and treatment.

To confuse expertise with perfection is dangerous in the extreme, whether in the operating room or the board room. We often fear a retribution that isn't present or likely, but sometimes we do react to curtness and impatience by holding our tongue. As a result, we're often left holding the bag.

We are inculcated with our *inferiority* in the presence of *experts*. In the third grade we had a visiting teacher ask us to name a word starting with "X." We proudly offered "xylophone," and the instructor informed us that our answer was wrong, since it started with a "Z!" That prompted a very early and fortunate cynicism about expertise based on title or rank (or even experience).

College professors adore the mantle of intellectual invincibility and law school professors seem to thrive on it. In fact, the narrower and tougher the specialty, the more imperial wisdom seems to be reserved for only the select few, and neophytes need to grovel in the presence of such gravitas. We recall a newly minted political science professor in a freshman class at Rutgers, outraged at students talking in the rear of the room, screaming, "Don't you know that you should never interrupt an urban intellectual when he's speaking!!"

Well, no, we didn't. It wasn't in the freshman handbook.

Profitable Language

When you vest someone else with superior powers of logic and speech, you diminish yourself. The most effective and profitable language involves mutual respect.

Examples of profitable language and mutual respect:

- Your point is well taken, and I think my view is supportive, though somewhat different. How can we best combine them? (Not: Would you be willing to combine them?)
- That's an unusual approach. Let's discuss the pros and cons since we've never attempted it before. (Not: I don't know what to say, I've never even considered that approach.)

- Please don't feel that we've ignored your suggestion. I'm prepared to adapt some of it and revisit the entire proposition at a later date. (Not: You were unprepared and your response shows it.)

Why do we hesitate to question at the most pertinent times and wind up bemoaning our timidity, languishing about what we "should have said," and "Why didn't I say …"? We've found the following elements at work, which are a lot more rational and manageable than fears of heights or public speaking or first dates:

- The insinuation that our questions are naïve or even stupid.
- The perception that we will lose respect by asking.
- The fear that we will antagonize someone with power over our future (health, graduation, advancement).
- The misbelief that we are under time pressure.
- The notion that our question has been answered and we missed or didn't understand the answer.
- Normative pressure in meetings from others who are also not asking questions.
- The fear of retribution (it's your fault, you can lead the committee, you go see the complaining client).
- Not being in the moment (distracted by something previously said, trying to formulate a future comment, and so forth).
- Poor self-esteem (they are more important than I am).

All of these steps are remedial, of course, and revolve around these basic approaches:

1. Prepare for the meeting or interaction when possible. What do you want to know about your condition, the decision, the objectives? Write down the concerns.
2. View the other person as a peer and coequal. You are both adults, and job titles, honorifics, and specialties don't change that immutable fact.

3. Focus on asking a specific question. Don't *think out loud.* Too many people articulate their cognitive processes, searching for meaning while they speak and driving those around them into semicomas. Practice being specific and succinct.

4. Remind yourself of the implications of *not* asking the question. Will you take the wrong route, study the wrong subject matter, arrive at the wrong time, lose the wrong kidney? These are far greater risks than a question being scoffed at.

5. Eschew perfection and infallibility. Satellites blow up on the launching pad, underdogs win ball games, no one can really time the stock market. Stop vesting others with talents and power they neither possess nor claim.

The first lesson in overcoming the hesitancy to question is to vest authority in yourself, not in others. Never begin by disempowering yourself!

The Mania of Perfection

The opposite of vesting others with infallibility is believing that we must possess it ourselves to be credible.

Our observation in all manner of organizations is that perfection is the arch enemy of excellence. People hesitate, invest too much time, check too many contingencies, and generally drag an anchor to try to ensure a project or decision is perfect before launching.

Which, of course, is abjectly impossible.

You have *never* been in a perfect plane, enjoyed a perfect meal, or experienced a perfect vacation. Imperfection is the norm, else, we wouldn't be able to walk erect. Baseball lore honors the *perfect game,* without a hit or walk, but the pitcher did throw balls (nonstrikes), and the ball was hit to the fielders. It seems to us that a *perfect game* would involve 81 pitches, three each to 27 batters who wouldn't touch any of them.

That, of course, will never be done. (If Sandy Koufax had a longer career, well, who knows?)

We seek perfection because we're afraid of others finding fault. We believe that errors and mistakes are commentaries on our self-worth rather than merely situational failures of attention or skills. (Whenever someone says, "I found four typos in your last book," we reflexively reply, "There were nine, you'd better have another look.") The U.S. Constitution has a bad slipup, not allowing women to vote, and God is often redundant in the Bible ("Take your two shoes off from both of your feet.")

Assembly lines and automation are intended to try to enhance the odds of perfection, yet we still have auto recalls and variances in fit between acceptable tolerances. Yet, the more access we have to more data, the more we tend to be highly imperfect.

Profitable Language

The future power is not in the hands of the diligently perfect, precise, and pontifical, but rather in those of leaders who can tolerate and act boldly in the midst of great ambiguity and doubt.

Examples of future power language and clarity:

- I'm not sure that we'll ever have all the information we'd like to have, but I am sure that if we don't move now, we'll never achieve the results we need to have.
- I'm responsible. We'll make midcourse corrections and adjust as we proceed. If we make errors along the way, so long as it's for a good cause and the right goal, no one will be criticized.
- Perfection undermines excellence. Let's make sure we're successful, not perfect.

In our blind search for and belief in perfectionism, we neglect to ask questions that we believe may not, themselves, be perfect. Hence, we may not ask if a car has a heated steering wheel (ideal for northeastern winters) because we believe the salesperson expects that we've already consulted the brochures and specs. We may not ask a question of the chief financial officer because she's an expert in finance and our question isn't likely to pass muster when her charts, boxes, and spreadsheets reek of perfection.

A Mars climate device crashed once because the two teams working on it—one in California and one in Colorado—both had perfect calculations and tolerances, which were approved. Of course, one team was working in inches and the other team in centimeters, which came to light only when the craft crashed into the planet after months in space and a cost of $125 million.

Perfectly screwed up.

You can observe the mania for perfection all around you, without anyone questioning whether the focus is worth it. People scrupulously attack stray weeds in a lawn, sweat over 1,000-page reports that may have the first few pages read but nothing more, use tiny cotton balls to clean remote nooks and crannies in their cars. Our fathers' advice was far more pragmatic and beneficial: When you buy a new car, find a place to kick it and create a slight scratch. You will then know it's no longer perfect, will know exactly where the imperfection is, and will no longer have to worry about it!

How can we kick the *perfection performance anxiety* issue? Fortunately, it's not difficult if you're willing to entertain slightly imperfect remedies:

1. Ask yourself what would be accepted as success by your intended audience (boss, spouse, customers, members, and so forth) and not what would constitute perfection.
2. When you're 80 percent ready, move. Understand that the final 20 percent heading toward *perfection* is not appreciated by the readers of a book, attendees at a speech, members of a committee, or clients of your firm.
3. We live in the age of speed. The dominant factor should be arriving with the best (not perfect) response before all others.
4. We prize resilience the most, the ability to bounce back, to score at the end of the game, to pull victory from the jaws of defeat, and react to unintended consequences.

Perfectionism is anathema to the language of profit. As a matter of fact, it is perfectly deadly.

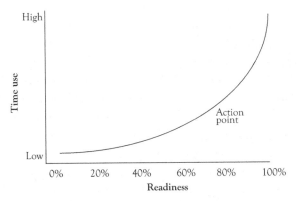

Figure 1.1 Move when 80 percent ready

The "What Do I Know?" Syndrome

There is an urban legend that the daily reader of *The New York Times* processes more information than an inhabitant of the 16th century processed in an entire lifetime. Even when considering the average lifespan to be about 33 years in the 1500s, that seems like a stretch, since it was a time of Copernicus, Da Vinci, Erasmus, and world exploration.

In fact, the issue today is the converse: We have so much more to know that we realize we know precious little. In the 16th century, one could be a polymath engaged in mathematics, physics, sailing, poetry, and anatomy. Today, we are highly specialized. (We met a doctor a while ago who did nothing but retinal work in premature babies. Football teams have separate coaches for receivers, linemen, linebackers, kickers, quarterbacks, and so on.)

As recently as the 1970s, one could evaluate for purchase fewer than 20 automobile marques, a dozen television manufacturers, and perhaps 10 kinds of coffee. Walk into a store such as Best Buy today and you're confronted with several hundred television screens with varied technology. Twenty years ago, there might have been five car choices in excess of $100,000, but today there are scores and Bentley is the most popular ultra-luxury car in the United States. A Starbucks will offer you a vente cappuccino, with soy milk, an extra shot of espresso, and cinnamon. Even the menu choices at a McDonald's drive-through are mind-boggling, and we often make a rash choice while concerned about holding up the line behind us for too long.

That apocryphal citizen of 500 years ago who had a decent education had a better grip on most of his or her universe than people today with a massive education have on theirs. (And the uneducated, agrarian worker back then had more control over his fate than the high school graduates laboring in offices today.) The problem we are experiencing today in ever-greater degree is "What do I know?"

The answer, when taken in the context of our global and technological existence, is *relatively little!*

That's not meant to be a concession or victimization statement. It is simply one of the underlying reasons that we don't always adapt the language of profit and too often rely on what we believe someone else *knows* rather than what we know or can find out.

A great many medical and nutrition experts maintain that we know our bodies best (as does the Bible, which first stipulated this in Corinthians two millennia ago). We've found in all kinds of organizations that there is a *business affinity* that people grow into enabling them to make intelligent, seemingly visceral decisions about the business every day, without formal instruction or methodology.

We know more than we think we do, we simply don't often recognize it, externalize it, or make it extrinsic. In their seminal work, *The Knowledge Creating Company* (Oxford University Press, 1995), Ikujiro Nonaka and Hirotaka Takeuchi make the case that intrinsic (inner) knowledge needs to be made extrinsic, and extrinsic (outer) knowledge needs to be made intrinsic. Thus, something you uniquely know of importance needs to be shared with colleagues, and something widely known in the company must become second-nature to you.

Even people with such business affinity and intrinsic–extrinsic knowledge tend not to appreciate how much they really know and, instead, often believe they know too little to make decisions effectively. Yet, they have all the power they need to ask the right questions, analyze the responses, and diagnose the situation in order to take effective and rapid action.

Yet they keep wondering, "What do I know?"

Counterintuitively, in an age of abundant choices, we are faced with a poverty of options. The more choices we have, the less likely we are to make one. Smart realtors focus on just a few factors important to the client (e.g., distance to school, view, safe neighborhood), as do auto dealers (fuel economy, cargo space, music system), as do investment specialists (liquidity, conservatism, safety). These factors differ from client to client, customer to customer, but the common issue is to *reduce the variables to a manageable few.*

Part of our hesitancy to question stems from the fear of not knowing enough, faced with so many options, that we simply ask nothing at all, believing that anything we ask will be inadequate. Women faced with breast cancer and men with prostate cancer diagnoses, under considerable strain and pressure, must decide among varied and often conflicting treatments, ranging from *watchful waiting* to highly intrusive surgeries and toxic chemicals.

Profitable Language

You know more than you think you do and you can find out what you need to if you focus on the language of inquiry and not on the fear of being seen as inadequate.

Examples of excellence in inquiry:

- Let's not be concerned with blame, let's find the cause of the problem, because we know this used to work, so something must have happened to stop it from working.
- We seem to be talking solely about benefits from this initiative and not considering whether there are relevant risks to take into consideration.
- We've prepared ourselves for setbacks, but not success. If this plan goes the way we intend it to, what will we then put in place to exploit our success, other than merely patting ourselves on the back? What's the equivalent of our next *app*?

We've seen people decide on an expensive house or car without doing much shopping because they simply want the experience to be over and escape from what seem like infinite choices. We've seen the same thing in boardrooms, where decisions to expand into new markets, or change the compensation system, or make an acquisition were made because conversations become circular and didn't advance a resolution. One executive told us, "We'll never have enough information, we can't verify everything, we often have to go with our gut."

That's fine for betting on football, but not for betting on the future of the enterprise.

Here's how to overcome the "What do I know?" syndrome of knowledge inadequacy:

1. Narrow your choices based on macrocriteria. Do you want a sports car or a family car? Do you prefer to vacation at the ocean or the mountains? Are you seeking more revenue from existing customers or more new customers?

2. Use others' experience for leverage. Don't become the test pilot, talk to those who have gone before you. What was their experience? What should you absolutely rule out? Henry Ford observed that if he had asked customers what they wanted, they would have said "faster horses." Does that apply to your business as well?

3. Codify your collective expertise. What do you know (market share)? What do you not know that you can find out (probable growth in market overall)? What do you not know that you probably will never know ahead of time (competition's new offerings)? Make your decisions based on what you do know and can find out as much as possible, not on what you don't know and can't find out.

4. Apply your judgment. Skills one can buy by the bushel, but judgment is a much rarer trait. If you see a television that is hard to adjust in the store, under optimal conditions, it will probably be even more difficult in your home. If you see other companies using a compensation system that has caused a decline in productivity, the chances are that it will do the same for you. You are not paid to take action, you are paid to achieve results.

This has been about "What do I know?" Our final segment refers more to "Whom do I know?"

Fear of Falling Off the Bandwagon

The bandwagon was, once, the wagon that carried the band during a parade. It was highly popular during political rallies, and onlookers would be encouraged to *jump on the bandwagon* to join the movement, and not to *fall off the bandwagon* and abandon the movement.

Psychologically, this represents strong normative (peer) pressure. Once something gains motion, the inertia is supportive of it remaining in motion, and popularity further and exponentially increases speed. We've seen this on huge scale with positive effect (landing a man on the moon within a decade as proclaimed by President Kennedy) and disastrous effect (investors frantically trying to gain the promised dramatic returns of Bernie Madoff's ultimate Ponzi Scheme).

In organizations and among individuals socially, normative or band-wagon pressure is one of the three major potential forces in behavior change (along with coercion at one extreme and enlightened self-interest at the other). Normative pressure (representing often artificial *norms* created by circumstances or arbitrarily by management) is highly effective and also quite fickle. The fashion industry is representative of the hairpin turns that hemlines, jacket styles, and accessories can maneuver from one season to the next.

Our hesitancy to question, undermining the language of profit, is often rooted in our frenzy to remain on the current bandwagon and being alert to jump on a newer, better one. We've seen organizations launch multimillion dollar campaigns with hardly a question raised about the consumers' reactions. (Remember the old dog food story about the ultimate cause of its failure, despite massive marketing resources, was that "the dogs just don't like the stuff?") As we write this, Victoria's Secret has had to embarrassingly end a huge advertising effort about its lingerie creating the *perfect body*. The problem was that women were outraged that the supermodels in the ads—who are about as common in American homes as silver mines—were cited as representing the *perfect body* for real, live women who had to raise children, work, and otherwise live their lives.

No one in the ad company or the organization's executive ranks in commissioning and approving the ad had asked that simple question of potential consumers: "How does the implication of this promotion strike you?" or "What feeling does this create for you?"

It's safe to say that *outrage* and *resentment* wouldn't have been what the company was looking for.

Profitable Language

Too often, our ability to question is dampened or squelched by our fears of being seen as not supporting the *in crowd* or backing the current initiative. We have to overcome affiliation needs by applying sound business needs.

Examples of standing apart from the crowd:

- Someone has to play *devil's advocate*, so let me take some opposing views and you fire back before we actually commit money and resources.
- The engineers who warned about faulty *O-rings* on the Shuttle Challenger were overruled by their superiors, and every one of them would love to be able to reverse that decision.
- We're all busy preaching to our own choir. Let's take this outside the company and get some reactions from both current customers and prospective customers.

We look around the bandwagon and see everyone else having a jolly good time, and the conveyance gaining speed. It's dangerous to jump off, and impossible to get back on even if you survive the fall. Of course, by jumping off you may survive the catastrophe when the entire initiative crashes.

For a long time, the *bandwagon* for cell phones was smaller and sleeker. Motorola was dominating the market when it introduced the *Razor*, the smallest and thinnest phone at that time. But both Samsung and Apple saw the future as smart phones, technologically driven and not cosmetically driven, and those two firms now own the market and Motorola has disappeared. (The recent IPhone 6+ is actually larger than anything yet produced, and the current movement is to a size between phones and tablets—*phablets*.)

The bandwagon had been toward reducing first-class seating in airplanes and substituting business and (much more) economy seating. However, following the lead of the giant competitors in the Emirates (Etihad, Emirates, and Qatar), airlines have turned to a renewed emphasis on first-class ground amenities and cabin services. The once-unrivaled upper class (business class) lounge of Virgin Air at Heathrow in London has been surpassed easily by the first-class *club* (an entire floor) of Emirates in Dubai, and that airline offers showers and private cabins on many first-class flights, while Etihad offers a sleeping suite with butler.

Following the pack does not allow for market dominance, nor does joining the pack on the bandwagon. The old organizational *yes man* has been resurrected as the unquestioning, don't-rock-the-boat supporter. Yet, this isn't what builds great organizations, which must rely on creative tension for innovation, nor successful individuals, who must remove themselves from the herd mentality.

We imply no great malice here. Organizational tropism tends to lean toward mutual support, suppressing dissonance, and demonstrating consensus and commitment. These are prized traits, rewarded formally and informally by management. The *team player* is much more desirable than the maverick in most organizations. But that *natural* proclivity toward harmony is dangerous and often dysfunctional because it prevents the kind of pointed, tough, and, ultimately, constructive questioning that might have prevented the launch of the doomed Challenger Space Shuttle, or the reliance on wholly inappropriate measures in New Orleans as Hurricane Katrina bore down, or the launching of any number of financially ruinous theatrical events.

Ultimately, we need to question why we're not questioning.

CHAPTER 2

Snarled in Data, Saved by Clarifying Language

Escaping from Our Own Nets

Second, the language of clarity: We need to extricate knowledge from information. Data should lead to information, which creates knowledge and, ultimately, wisdom. Yet data (let along "big data") too often confuses and obfuscates. This chapter deals with the best methods to speak and write about data and turn it into highly useful information, applicable knowledge, and even profound wisdom.

Analytic Arabesques

An *arabesque* is a dance position where the dancer precariously supports a movement on one leg, while the other is extended horizontally ... oh, and also backward.

An *arabesque* is also an ornamental design consisting of intertwined and flowing lines, often found in Moorish and Arabic decoration. Visiting Istanbul recently, I saw these in every possible artistic combination in many mosques. The design often features interlacing foliage and tendrils.

Enough for our arts program. The point is that language often becomes this contorted, this confusing, this dazzling to the receiver. We have the luxury of reflecting upon art, but not so much so while trying to rapidly and effectively communicate.

The arabesques we speak of are those where we advertently or inadvertently distort meaning by creating convoluted patterns with the language. This is exacerbated by technology and unemotional, one-dimensional e-mail as a primary communications form (we'd rate texting as 0.5 dimensional, in case you're wondering).

A brief example is the feigned aesthetic of the television news reporter who says "Between you and I ..." because it seems so decorous, even if every educated person knows it's also wrong.* It's like sniffing a wine cork, which does you as much good as licking the label in terms of evaluating the wine. It is an affectation.

We can watch arabesques create the more colloquial *foot in mouth* syndrome (think about the position, also very difficult to maintain), when very little thought is invested in the beginning of the sentence so that there is no control whatsoever in terms of the landmines, dead ends, and general wrecks it may encounter by its termination. Then there is FIMR, foot-in-mouth recovery, which always makes things worse.

Here is the conversation in a select, wealthy group's cocktail party prior to an important meeting:

Suzie: So, Gunther, I'm impressed with your success. You can't be older than 54.

Gunther: (Outraged) Did you say 54!? I'm 48! How can you think I'm 54? Everyone tells me I don't look my age!

Suzie: I didn't mean to say you look older than you are, only that you're so well groomed and dressed that you look even better than you otherwise, well, I mean, no one would know just by looking at you, but I know because we've talked before ...

You get the idea. It's like finding yourself on thin ice when you happen to be carrying a flamethrower, and then you inexplicably turn it on and point it at your feet.

The arabesque happens so often in our language because we're snarled in data. We find ourselves in painful and contorted positions because we don't know what to disregard or what to cull out, so we try to make sense of it all. That's why we wind up looking like a pretzel.

This is the usual sequence we've found that creates great power:

Data ... information ... knowledge ... wisdom

Nothing fancy there. But a lot that may be hidden can undermine us.

---

* "Between" is a preposition which takes the objective form, "me," not the nominative form, "I." We learned that in sixth grade.

Profitable Language

Keep it simple is no longer sufficient. *Keep is accurate and brief* is the new rule.

For example, we tend to *spew* analytics like an erupting volcano because:

- We make the mistake believing that *data speaks for itself*.
- We have overconfidence in research, or what passes for research, especially when it appears to support our own conclusions and biases.
- We have a burning desire to impress others!

Let's define terms:

Data: Units of statistics, numbers, words, and language that can be gathered and sorted.

Information: Facts derived from data that can be verified and validated.

Knowledge: Information combined with one's talents that creates a grasp of subject matter, context, and application.

Wisdom: Information combined with judgment and experience to anticipate and apply solutions and make quality decisions.

Whether you agree with our precise definitions or not, the key is to understand that the terms imply different meanings and they occur in a certain sequence. We don't believe it's an accident that people can talk about *smart people*, but you seldom hear them refer to *wise people*.

Therefore, data without interpretation, validation, and relevance is useless or, at best, peripheral. It can confuse and obfuscate if it isn't culled and disregarded. While we often focus on the art and science of presenting information, we seldom focus on *what* information really constitutes. (At this writing, there is a huge controversy about the wisdom of vaccinating children against measles, pitting scientific wisdom on one side and misinformation on the other.) We'll deal more with this later in this chapter.

Data tends to be quantitative, emphasizing amounts, degree, scope, and so forth. But information that is gleaned from it begins the qualitative transformation to knowledge. What are our options? What are our risks? Who should be involved?

In 1989, a telecommunication firm introduced a new 800 (toll-free) product for small business and residential use (they were breaking ground in the industry with residential 800 plans). Many hours were invested in brainstorming and think tanks, along with advertising and branding consultations. The powers to be selected: 1-800-FREEDOM, with the accompanying red, white, and blue all-American theme. Marketing just needed to make sure that number wasn't in use by an existing organization.

The director of product management immediately had his team on the data search. The data analyst spent days pulling data reports. They were like a pack of dogs digging for that one bone. (Remember, 1980s were the peak of greenbar, hardcopy data reports.)

Based on the data, 1800FREEDOM was available, and was blessed as the new product name and promotion. It was approved and printed on everything from marketing collateral to pens and hats, and any other tchotchke that 1800FREEDOM would fit on. The new product was rolled out and introduced with grand fanfare.

It didn't take long for the call to come in. The call came from a business customer … the Freedom Group, which had owned 1800FREEDOM for a few years.

The devastated and demoralized product director went to the Marketing VP's office, with reams of green bar reports in tow, citing his defense of, "But, with all of this extensive data research, the number never once showed up." Without hesitation, the VP vociferously challenged, *"Did you ever consider picking up the '*#@?!' phone and dialing the number to see if someone answered???"*

Knowledge and wisdom (along with what could be viewed as *common sense*) trump data. Or, if you think you have the right answer, wait to see if someone answers.

When Everything Is a Priority Nothing Is a Priority

People are fond of pointing out that a photo of Einstein's desk on the day he died reveals a profusion of books, papers, and notes apparently randomly scattered. They use this as proof that great minds need not be organized.

Don't confuse a filing system (or lack of one) with the ability to set priorities. The theory of relativity didn't emerge by accident from a warren of pigeonholes on Einstein's desk.

Priority (and it's formerly ungrammatical lovechild, *prioritize*) means "to establish what things are more important than other things." In all candors, can you answer easily how that's done in your life and your business?

How are priorities set in your organization? Who sets them? What criteria are used? How is the *what and why* (the expected end result and value) communicated? Ideally, priorities are in direct alignment with the organization's strategy. Too often, that's not the case. Frequently, priorities are set by what appears to be the whim of those with the *loudest voice*. More times than not, this would be a person of *authority*.

From the early days of apprenticeship through the Industrial Revolution, the person(s) in charge charted the path, barked the orders related to their own agendas, and expected everyone to fall in line to implement and execute accordingly. Others (even at an executive level) weren't asked for their insights or contributions. In fact, the common cliché of old, "I didn't ask you to think. Just do what I tell you to do," was rampant. (The modern form, often issued by parents to argumentative children, is, "Do as I say, not as I do.")

The opposite extreme of this autocratic priority setting is equally ineffective and damaging. This is where priority setting becomes decision by committee or a consensus process. There are hours and days of brainstorming and collaborative think-tank conversations in hopes of obtaining everyone's buy-in so everyone leaves *deliriously happy* as to the game plan.

Case Study

When I worked with Hewlett-Packard a decade ago, I found that the meetings were incredibly harmonious. Yet, nothing was really accomplished since the *harmony* was about very superficial issues.

I found out later that there was a series of *pre-meeting meetings* to ensure that nothing unharmonious caused confrontation or conflict. In order to get past this insistence on harmony as a priority—instead of progress as the priority—we invented the phrase, "Putting the dead rat on the table."

Sadly, even when priorities are properly designated and aligned with strategy, they may morph or contort as they trickle through the functions and levels of an organization. They can get lost, confused, railroaded, undermined, and forgotten (or worse yet, totally ignored). So, too, with our individual priorities as we face the unanticipated issues that surface during our day.

The key questions here are, "As a leader, how *should* you effectively lead the prioritization process, which is a vital and critical leadership skill in setting, aligning, and implementing priorities? What language is useful in accomplishing this?" The answer lies in the following subsets:

- How should priorities be set in your organization?
- Who should set them?
- What criteria should be used?
- What language will aid and abet the process and ensure success?

Profitable Language

Setting priorities is dependent on the criteria you choose and agreement on those criteria. Hence, language supporting the criteria must be simple and clear.

Setting priorities in a crisis is similar to triage in a medical setting. In any television hospital drama, everyone on the medical staff immediately stopped what they were doing and positioned for triage as mass accident victims arrive. Injuries are assessed and classified on a spectrum from superficial to life threatening. The drama is indicative of medical triage in real life.

Triage, comes from the French phrase *trier*, meaning to *select or sort out*. Triage is, by definition, "the assignment of degrees of urgency to wounds or illnesses to decide the order of treatment of a large number of patients or casualties." It is a standardized process and system *of priorities* to be used in an emergency or crisis situation. In the world of medicine, it is based on the very fact that if everything is a priority, then nothing is a priority. (To put it another way, you may be successfully applying band aids to some, thinking you're successful, while others are dying.)

Triage is a contingent action. It answers the question, "Once the damage has occurred, how do we best deal with it (fix or mitigate it) in the moment and what is the order (priority) of immediate and next-step actions?"

There is a time and place for the concept of triage in any element of a crisis in any type of setting. However, prioritization should be a *proactive approach*. It is intended to successfully chart a path. It creates a road map to *get from here to there* most expeditiously.

Let's explore how you, as an effective leader, can master the art of prioritization proactively and preventively. Setting priorities isn't rocket science, but there is a method and a system to the language.

To be proactive and not in the crisis triage mode, you need criteria in advance. We'll suggest three that we've found to be simple and clear:

- *Seriousness:* What is the gravity or impact of the issue? *Low* may represent a minor disturbance, *medium* requires damage control or immediate action, and *high* could be a dramatic, organizationwide outcome. (Low could be a person resigning unexpectedly, medium the chance to gain a new client, and high an acquisition, for example.)
- *Urgency:* What is the compelling need to act quickly? *Low* may mean that you clearly have time without worsening affects, *medium* means that you have a definite window for action, and *high* means that you need to act immediately to seize an opportunity or to extinguish a fire.
- *Growth*: Is the situation improving, stable, or declining?

With this language we can make a simple chart*:

	Issue 1	Issue 2	Issue 3	Issue 4
Seriousness				
Urgency				
Growth				

---

* You can substitute 10-1 or whatever scoring you prefer if "high, medium, and low" aren't precise enough for your purposes.

There's no such thing as a stupid question, right? Wrong! There are plenty of stupid questions being asked. If you ask the wrong question— use the wrong language—you're never going to get the right information. Hence, we've restricted our proactive priority setting to the clear and simple:

"What is the level of seriousness?" "What is your evidence?"

To that point, one aspect of the language of success is how you respond to questions being asked of you. Leaders are prepped, prompted, and promoted on their ability to respond and tell. Thinking quickly on your feet and not hesitating with a response is thought to be a sign of confidence and conviction. And, yet, the true language of success is not merely how good you are at telling and responding to questions. The language of success includes how talented you are at *asking* questions (especially of others and often of yourself) in order to gain relevant and pertinent information.

When it comes to setting priorities, leaders need to know when to tell and when to ask. And, more importantly, leaders need to be masters at *asking the right questions at the right time.* (There will be more on critical questioning skills in Chapter 4.)

Information Isn't Knowledge

People are generally applauded for responding and reacting quickly—"thinking quickly on their feet, turning around on a dime, taking action immediately." Often, the focus is acknowledgment of the immediate action, regardless of whether the desired results are achieved. I once took on a pharmaceutical consulting firm as a client to find that they applauded themselves on grinding out 30 proposals a month—but no one tracked their business closing rate! (Granted, there's a time and place when information must be quickly assessed and immediate action is warranted—such as triage or crisis intervention. In those circumstances, the focus is taking the right action in order to obtain the best outcomes or results.)

At the opposite end of the spectrum, we deal with the scenario of *analysis paralysis.* Information is mined, collected, dissected, and regurgitated. It is profusely spouted and spewed like Mt. Vesuvius hovering over

Pompei and Herculaneum. And, yet, knowledge may never be achieved through the grinding friction of never-ending analysis.

In any circumstance, acting on information without sufficient knowledge can be destructive and deadly (figuratively and literally). What are the right amounts of alchemy? What is too much or too little? The key is that amount which transforms information into knowledge.

Profitable Language

"Do we have enough information to make an intelligent decision?" is the wrong question. The correct question is "Do we have enough knowledge to make an intelligent decision?"

The pathway of information to knowledge is highly dependent on how we consciously and unconsciously obtain, filter, and process information. Everyone is subject to biased thinking and processing based on beliefs and experiences.

The following are some criteria to use to ensure that you're using the language of success and not failure in three critical areas:

- Avoid confirmation bias: Confirmation bias is the tendency to search for, translate, interpret, and generally apply information only insofar as it is consistent with our personal predispositions and beliefs. We find this with global warming debates, as each *side* uses only reports, scientists, analyses, and comparisons that support its position (and, hence, a scandal that crops up every so often on falsified *research*).

  In business, we need to search for and combine information based on empirical reality and evidence, not merely that which supports our position. We're not on a debate team or trying to convince a jury as a defense attorney.

- Avoid recency bias: This is the tendency to believe the first or last things in a series as best, and those items in the middle the least. Pragmatically, it's the phenomenon in business of *getting the boss's ear last.*

  In a luxury hotel, no matter how much is spent on lavish décor or amenities, for front desk speed, the greatest impression is created by the doorman—the very first person and the very last person a guest encounters. That's fine for hotels if their doorman is outstanding, but hardly the return on investment (ROI) sought for the property.

We need to train ourselves to consider the *entire* path and flow of information as we create knowledge, not just the last thing we've been exposed to. This is especially true in strategy. Recency bias creates very poor chess players, who tend to focus only on the prior move of the opponent and not its implications six moves hence.

- Avoid illusory correlation: This is the false connection of otherwise legitimate information in flawed etiology. It is the erroneous perception that two unrelated events are related.

  In sports, a new coach's winning season often ignores the prior coach's carefully laid plans for the future (the Tampa Bay Buccaneers won a Super Bowl after firing Tony Dungy, who had laid all the groundwork, and who would win a future Super Bowl with the exact same preparation in Baltimore).

  People have tended to connect performance with higher pay, yet countless studies have shown that performance most relies on autonomy and pride in one's work. The danger with illusory bias in business with this issue, for example, is that if you pay an unhappy employee more money, you simply have a wealthier, unhappy employee!

Even empirical evidence (experience or observable behavior) is subject to and influenced by our own biases.

When taking action, why are we *sure* we have the right answer and then turn out to be wrong? After the fact, people are quick to reply in defense of their ineffective actions, "We didn't have the right information, or enough information, or we didn't trust the information we had." In reality, it's seldom about the raw information. It's typically due to *a lack of knowledge* by those making the decisions.

Case Study

Radio Shack, an early innovator in home computers and consumer electronics, declared bankruptcy and went out of business in 2015.

They had tried to revive their plummeting sales with remote control toys and replacements for broken screens on mobile devices. This failed miserably.

The management of Radio Shack had vast information on its customers and their buying habits, a huge method of distribution, and overwhelming information about current consumer trends and successes (Apple) and failures (RIM). Yet, they didn't combine the information into useful and accurate knowledge, or they would have changed their name (*radio* in 2015?), attempted a merger using their vast network of stores as an asset for distribution, and performed triage on their retail operation.

Many years ago, Penn Central was hemorrhaging money as a railroad, when its management looked at the company with the underappreciated knowledge that it had vast land holdings because of historical government grants in building tracks across the country.

It sold the railroad and went into the real estate business, and became quite profitable.

Years after that, struggling Pan American Airlines sold its iconic office building in the heart of Manhattan to help support the failing airline. In hindsight, it should have sold the airline and kept the building.

I attended an ethics discussion years ago to which two dozen tough executives were invited by an ethics foundation. The guest speaker was at first halting stumbling, and you could feel the disappointment in the room. And he kept fidgeting with a piece of rubber he had brought with him.

In 1986, the Challenger Space Shuttle disaster,—the information and evidence regarding the O-rings were there. Based on the known information, the knowledge was known by those who escalated the concern. This man before us was one of those engineers begging his supervision to delay the launch.

But that knowledge was not accepted and absorbed by those in authority positions, those who made the ultimate call of *go or no go*. The knowledge was ignored (discounted or dismissed) with devastating results. The Challenger disaster resulted in a 32-month hiatus in the shuttle program. The Rogers Commission, assigned to determine *cause*, focused on the technology of the compromised O-rings.

But, ultimately, the commission found NASA's organizational culture and decision making were key contributing factors to the accident. They accepted information supportive of their positions, but rejected others' knowledge that contradicted it. That was a disaster. But every day, this same phenomenon is dooming business decisions, undermining profit, and sidetracking success.

Knowledge Isn't Wisdom

We're now at the ultimate bastion of the language of success: wisdom. Wisdom is the ability to apply one's experience, education, knowledge, talent, and judgment to an issue in order to solve, improve, create, innovate, and so forth.

Wisdom can also be considered as a body of knowledge that develops within institutional and historical basis for conveying successful and positive values and lessons from one generation to the next. There is wisdom in families, schools, neighborhoods, organizations, and cultures.

In Figure 2.1, we can see the components of wisdom in a more formalized fashion and how they interrelate.

Figure 2.1 Wisdom pyramid

At the lowest level, we all have experiences that help form our lives and beliefs. Those vary from person to person, and are affected by geography, parents, affluence or poverty, environment, and so forth. Next is education, which may be formal or informal, and may range from relatively little to higher degrees. Then we have talent, which is often changing in many of us, as we grow passionate or grow bored, as we have the opportunity to learn and experiment or are stultified. Many of you reading this are refugees from large companies (or wish to become refugees) because you feel entrapped and constrained. Realizing one's talents, and being recognized for them, is a key component of employee motivation, as we discussed earlier. These are not strictly correlated with size. Large companies, for example, Apple or FedEx, can create productive and rewarding corporate cultures, while some entrepreneurs find themselves miserable because they have become lone wolves without affiliation needs being met and without external regard for their work.

Following that there is knowledge, which we described earlier as the intelligent assembly of information, gained by experience and education and the exercise of one's talents over time.

We next have judgment, which is an accrual of the prior factors. Judgment tends to improve as experiences and opportunities to try one's talents improve. Educations tend to improve judgment as well. Whether taking the potentially game winning shot with a second on the clock or deciding whether to launch a new product in the coming year, judgment is aided by familiarity and a sense of comfort. Launching the invasion of Normandy on the last day that the tide permitted in June with risky weather was a command decision of Dwight Eisenhower's based solely on his judgment.

Thus, the apex is wisdom, the capacity to apply these various factors with great power and focus to a single issue or a complexity of issues.

Profitable Language

We tend to denigrate *wise*, as in calling a smart aleck a *wise guy*, or referring to mobsters as *wise guys*. The real problem is a dearth of *wise* people.

How does this work in practice? Let's start at the *beginning*. The Magi were called *wise men* from the East. (It's thought they might actually have been early astronomers tracking a bright star.) They decided, despite King Herod's invitation, to avoid seeing him after seeing the baby Jesus and took another route because they wisely thought he wanted to do the infant harm. According to the Bible, that just might have created an important step for humankind.

Let's move from the sublime to the entirely pragmatic: Uber. Uber's founders took a common need (urban transportation) with a mediocre current solution (dirty, poorly maintained cabs that often stank) and employed technology (GPS and apps) to create what is currently an operation rapidly spreading globally and with a capitalized worth of over $40 billion—larger than 359 of the 469 publicly traded companies in the Fortune 500!

That was nothing as *simple* as creativity or a good idea. It was wise. The knowledge of the market and technology, talents of the founders, experiences of the public, and terrific judgment created this new behemoth.*

The reaction of the National Football League to physical assaults by its players has not been wise. It has left almost everyone without a feeling of closure or confidence. The owners and commissioner were hardly the Magi.

The shutdown for certain periods of Boston's mass transit system (trains, trolleys, buses) was not wise, even though it may have been deemed safe. How can we say that? Because the management *knew*—had the knowledge—that the system was old (one of the oldest in the United States), that the winters can be severe, and that its shutdown would strand tens of thousands. Yet, the management went blithely on (the general manager resigned after one blizzard in 2015) as if this knowledge wasn't enough for a call to action, just as the O-ring warnings weren't enough to prevent a tragedy.

---

* Judgment isn't always perfect. While Uber's strategy was spot on, they made major implementation and execution mistakes in not being more careful in screening its drivers during its rapid expansion, resulting in assaults, rapes, and lawsuits.

What language do you need to create and perpetuate wisdom? The following are our *wise* suggestions:

- What are my options in terms of what we know (instead of jumping to an arbitrary action)?
- Do I have all the information I need? If not, do I know what's missing and how to get it (the key ingredient for knowledge)?
- What can I use from my own experiential base—and from those I trust around me—to assist in this decision?
- Are there models or precedents in my past?
- What is the maximum upside (benefit) and downside (risk)? How can I exploit the former and mitigate the latter?
- On balance, what is the best outcome to be achieved within reasonable risk limits and with minimal or zero unvalidated assumptions?

Let's turn now to the bulwark of wisdom: truth.

CHAPTER 3

Truth or Consequences

Honesty Is Moral but Truth Is Pragmatic

Third, the language of the truth: There may be "lies and damn lies" but there is, more critically "truth and real truth." "Honesty" connotes a moral position, but truth denotes an empirical reality, which is owed to our employees, customers, investors, suppliers, families, and ourselves. Unfortunate choices of language can turn truths into lies and undermine honest communication.

Honesty Is Usually Subjective

Is a myth true or false? Is it *honest* or *dishonest*? Suppose I told you that a myth is a kernel of truth wrapped in a teaching lesson. Would that change your mind?

Is it *honest* to withhold information? Is the absence of the truth (versus an out and out lie or misrepresentation) being dishonest?

When we speak of honesty, we're speaking in highly subjective terms. We're dishonest about the existence of Santa Claus because we want our children to enjoy the thrill and excitement. It's the same with the tooth fairy. In a more serious vein, the Japanese seldom talk of *cancer* to family members, with the complicity of doctors, preferring to pretend the patient's illness is treatable.

Simon Cowell, the infamous judge of American Idol in the UK and United States, would preface critical remarks with, "If I'm really being honest ...," which implies that we often aren't when we're giving feedback. One of the greatest coaching issues among executives is helping them to provide honest feedback to subordinates during evaluation sessions (as well as all year long). In job interviews, the interviewer is often as afraid of rejection as the interviewee, creating hesitancy and less than full disclosure by both parties.

That's one of the reasons that hiring is more of a crapshoot than a science.

We make judgments all the time about what circumstance requires honesty and what requires a bit of dissembling. We see examples in sports—short of the actual cheats, steroid users, and so forth—where injuries are faked and bad calls accepted. (There is more acting in soccer games than in Hollywood.) People cheat and lie and ignore convenient truths, on the playing field, in their homes, and in their businesses.

But they don't see it as lying or fibbing or prevaricating because they rationalize the need, just as myths are used to convey values and lessons across generations, and need to be somewhat embellished to be effective. As a keynote speaker, I've often edited the facts in some of my stories to make the lessons more powerful. However, I've also had the wisdom to do this only when performing on a stage and not on my résumé!

Profitable Language

No one can avoid being dishonest at times by commission or omission, but we can make intelligent judgments about where it is for others' benefit and where it is simply for our own self-aggrandizement.

Brian Williams, the once exalted and then disgraced anchor on the NBC evening news was dishonest about his exploits in covering foreign battles, and perhaps elsewhere. What would have been acceptable at a small party over drinks was a cause for removal on the airways. He told his dishonest, embellished stories so often to so many that I'm convinced he actually began to believe them.

Honesty is usually subjective. Dishonesty is equally subjective (contrary to popular belief, it's not an absolute either). Consider the following common phrases that are all too familiar:

- "He did the only right and honest thing."
- "She made an honest mistake."
- "I haven't been totally honest with you about how I feel."

Honesty connotes sincerity, morality, decency, respectability, and virtuousness. While any and all of those may be desirable attributes, they are each subjective in nature and are based on perception and perspective.

Perception is how we understand or interpret something. (We're all familiar with the phrase "perception is reality.") Perspective is a particular attitude toward that understanding or interpretation. The very nature of differing perceptions and perspectives creates differing realities, and honesty.

Truth, however, *is* objective. Truth signifies an empirical reality. It is the heart of the scientific method.

In his initial reporting of the incident in 2003, Brian Williams recounted the combat story accurately and truthfully. In reports later that year, the story began to morph. By 2007, Williams recounted that he witnessed the chopper in front of him being hit, which was untrue. (The chopper ahead of him was hit, but William's chopper was 30 minutes behind, so it was impossible for him to have witnessed the hit.) In 2013, William now claimed the actual chopper he was riding in was hit (an even larger untruth).

Interestingly, Williams didn't manufacture the story from the beginning. It evolved and morphed as time went on. Each time he told the story, he made the circumstances more dangerous and became more of a *survivor*. He started with the truth and altered the course of his career (along with his credibility) with a lie that he continued to promote over a decade.

You may remember a similar story by Hillary Clinton while running for President in 2008. Clinton claimed she landed in Bosnia under sniper fire in1996 and had to run for cover with her head down. This was untrue (as documented by video) and she later rescinded the story. Even though it was media fodder at the time, the story quickly dissipated. Why the difference in outcomes in the two stories? Politicians are known for such stories. Journalists are expected to accurately (factually and truthfully) report the news.

How and why do these distinctions apply to leaders and the language of success? Why is truth imperative for leaders, whether it's finding it or communicating it? How do leaders capture and disseminate empirical reality?

Should we hold some to higher standards (reporters) than others (politicians)? How important is it to have the right language and methods to pursue the actual truth? I think it's vital in any business, any family, any community, and any relationship.

How to Distill the Truth

In Chapter 2, we stated, "It's not always about having the right answer. It's about asking the right question at the right time." (You'll notice it's a reoccurring theme throughout the book!) When it comes to distilling the truth, that guideline applies here as well. What questions need to be explored in order to determine empirical evidence?

Every journalist and investigator is taught the basics of "The Five Ws and How:" who, what, when, where, why, and how. From a journalistic and investigative perspective, these questions are usually posed in the past tense to determine circumstances and factual information:

- *Who* did that?
- *What* happened?
- *When* did it take place?
- *Where* did it take place?
- *Why* did that happen?
- *How* did it happen?

Whether posed as past, present, or future tense, none of these questions can be answered with a simple *yes* or *no*. *The very nature of these questions positions the respondent to offer information that will lead to evidence in the environment, also known as "the truth."*

Even though you ask the right questions, the respondents may not directly answer the question you asked. This can occur because they don't understand what you've asked, they misinterpret what you asked, or they are offering information that is a tangent to what you've asked. They may offer more or less information than what you need. And, they may have a private agenda that colors their *facts*.

Profitable Language

Opinions are often valuable, but you can put evidence in the bank. Make sure you're not trying to stash counterfeit language.

When seeking the truth, be cautious of responses that focus on blame, opinions, or disguised solutions, instead of factual information. The following are examples of each:

- Q: "What are the current annual sales numbers compared to quota?"
- A1: "Sales are below quota because the new product isn't well received by our customers" (*blame* and *opinion*)
- A2: "We need to do additional training on the new products to get the sales numbers up" (*disguised solution*)
- A3: "We're currently at 78 percent of quota for YTD sales" (*factual*)

Compare: Do you love me?

- How could I not love you? (evasive)
- As much as I know what love is? (conditional)
- Why do you ask me that now? (avoidance)
- Yes (but doesn't act it—dissonant)
- Yes (and acts it—factual)

In distilling the truth (mining for factual information), leaders need to:

1. Ask the right questions at the right time.
2. Assess and interpret the answers for fact, blame, opinion, and disguised solutions.
3. In the absence of factual information, continue to probe (restate or paraphrase) until the facts are offered.

There are times when you want factual information and there are times to ask people for their opinions. It may be to explore their ideas or suggestions to include them in determining the cause of a problem or looking for proposed solutions. We'll discuss these specific questioning techniques and language skills in Chapters 4, 5, and 6.

In some situations, distilling the truth is a matter of observation with an acute awareness and little or no conversation required. As a consultant and an executive coach, I routinely shadow my clients to observe them in action—conference calls, internal meetings, presentations, client interactions, and evaluation sessions. I also observe and listen to communications, interactions, and processes within and throughout a team, a department, or an entire organization.

What does one look for in regard to observed behavior in the environment? Whether in the role of a consultant or that of a leader, we're looking for the same empirical reality, the same truth through observation. To understand the value of empirical evidence, let's look at three very common ways leaders attempt to distill the truth:

1. *A Priori*: Relating to or denoting reasoning or knowledge that is determined from theoretical deduction instead of from observation or experience. There must be a force that causes all things dropped to head toward the surface and not toward the sky (and we know that force as gravity).
2. *Self-Reported Behavior*: A report of one's behavior provided by the subject who is demonstrating the behavior, such as "I never seem able to give someone what I consider negative feedback because I perceive that I am hurting, not helping them."
3. *Empirical Evidence*: Relying on or derived from observation or rather than theory. "Our customers are complaining that they cannot reach live service agents on the phone."

Of the three, empirical evidence via observation is the best means to truly determine the truth. Let's look at a simple scenario for the purpose of example:

Situation 1: Are employees following the newly defined and implemented procedures?

1. *A Priori*: Most employees typically follow every new process we implement. We have no reason to expect that behavior to change now. So, we conclude that they are following the new procedure.
2. *Self-Reported Behavior*: The employees say they are following the new procedures, so they must be.
3. *Empirical Evidence*: What do you actually observe? What are you seeing and hearing?

Observed behavior is the most reliable, with one significant caveat—that the observer is doing so through an *unbiased lens*. Your personal and professional biases can influence how you process the observed behavior and the conclusions you draw from those observations. (Note: We discussed biases in Chapter 2 and they apply here as well.)

What do you focus on during these observations? Depending on the circumstances, observations can be based on quantitative or qualitative behaviors. Examples include:

- Are most people doing this most of the time?
- Is it being done as described or in some other manner?
- Are we obtaining the results we anticipated?

Throughout these observations, you become aware of patterns, trends, and one-off behaviors (based on circumstances and variables). As a consultant and coach, I process this information constantly. As a leader, you can learn to do the same.

In the same way that big data focuses on predictive analytics, we can draw a parallel regarding observed behavior. We can predict the expected future behavior based on patterns of past performance and similar future scenarios. It's not an exact science to bank on, but it is worth projecting and speculating. "What got you here won't get you there" isn't always true.

Creating a Reliance on Evidence

There is a classic teaching device used in law school in the first year (I attended one week before deciding that the law was the equivalent of the rules of golf in its contradictions but not as reliant on honor) where a room of 100 students is suddenly confronted with an intruder rushing in from a side entrance. The intruder hits the professor and runs out the other side of the room.

The *eyewitness* accounts vary extremely among the class in terms of height, coloring, weight, and sometimes even gender. The point, of course, is that the vaunted *eyewitness testimony* is not all that reliant. (Think of how many *eyewitness news teams* there are branding themselves as such across the country.)

Evidence must be provable, validated, reliable, and, if possible, replicable. This is most probably when you have a pattern, which can be traced and expected to repeat. It's most difficult when you have only random occurrences. Serial killers are often caught because the advertently or inadvertently create a pattern, but many deliberately try to create seemingly random crimes.

Case Study

I was walking through a plant with the president and his top team as they dutifully examined the Six Sigma quality results listed at each station and machine, with the operator's explanation. I found little of it directly related to productivity and performance, statistical niceties that actually diverted attention.

I looked around and saw, across the floor, a steady flow of oil from a machine onto the surface. When I pointed this out to one of the executives in the entourage, he shushed me, saying, "We can get to that later, now we're focusing on the mandatory weekly metrics."

Meanwhile, oil leaked.

There are honest differences in perspective even among highly respected, honest, experienced people. Those differences can emanate from position, culture, gender, experiences, suppositions, agendas, and expectations—you get the idea. Thus, the *he said–she said* phenomenon, while cute in books and television comedies, must be avoided in business and important social contexts.

Another obstacle is wordplay. If we return to the law for a moment, there is a famous axiom: "When you have the merits, argue the merits.

When you don't have the merits, argue the law." Many cases are won and lost not on truth, but on technicalities and verbal gymnastics. At meetings, we've all experienced someone who carries the day through volume, or humor, or visual aids, or bluster, but not through the truth. Afterward, people wonder how they arrived at such a dreadful course of action.

There are also the people who willfully ignore evidence because it is inconvenient. Bernie Madoff's Ponzi scheme was implausible on the face of it—overly dramatic returns in a poor economy. But so long as some people received early money, everyone convinced themselves that it was okay, despite defying reality. And note that some very experienced and sophisticated investors were *self-duped* by this. Bernie was a con man, but he needed a very susceptible and not too scrutinizing a victim.

Profitable Language

Ask yourself how you would prove it and whether it can be replicated. Or, ask others. If you can't prove it or replicate it, it probably just ain't so.

The following are the questions that will help determine whether you have evidence to rely on:

- Have I observed and replicated cause and effect? (The stock market tends to rise and fall with the results of some NFL Super Bowl conference winners, but that's like determining that the economy usually improves when it rains.) When we deliver something by truck is it usually damaged, and by rail usually never damaged?
- Do independent sources validate the phenomenon? Our impression is that our customers are happy with us and that our 8 percent attrition rate is below average for our industry, but what would an independent agency or consultant find? (In a famous study, advertising agencies found that their clients thought more highly of their work than they, themselves, did, which adversely affected pricing and profit.)
- Am I observing an accident, coincidence, or trend? Too many people adjust their businesses, their lives, and their results

based on one-off feedback. (I always have someone unhappy with room temperature in conferences, but I'm not making a change when 200 other people are happy.) A pattern generally is occurring after three independent occurrences. Ignore anything short of that in terms of reliable evidence (or feedback).

- Is there a personal agenda that influences what I'm hearing and seeing? Defense lawyers don't pursue the *truth*, they pursue the acquittal of their client. (They call them *courts of law* not *courts of justice*.) Am I listening to a terribly sincere person who is zealous about a personal matter, not an organizational one? Is someone generalizing from a specific: "Mary didn't make the sale yesterday, hence, she needs more sales training," thus said the training director.

We've seen some lost airplanes over the past couple of years, and the causes are most reliably explained by examining the *black box* objective data, and turning it into useful information, and then knowledge of the crash conditions. We are then wiser about prevention in the future. (Air speed indicators can ice up and give false readings, creating stall conditions if the pilots are merely relying on autopilot alone.)

Businesses don't have *black boxes*, so we have to replicate objective information through the questions we ask and the weight we give to the answers. No one says, "We think the plane ran out of fuel, so let's increase the size of fuel tanks on the planes." Yet, we see some of this nonevidentiary, expensive behavior in many places. A nightclub fire in Rhode Island forced all small businesses to spend millions on different safety standards, yet the cause of the fire and lost life was negligence of the nightclub owners in not following existing standards. We continue to tighten drunk driving tolerances and arrests, yet the evidence is that a small minority of chronic offenders—usually with no insurance and no licenses in violation of existing laws—cause more of the accidents because they aren't held for a long term in prison and are consistent repeat offenders.

Discipline yourself to focus on evidence and ask the right questions to discover it. Recognize subterfuge and distraction, whether deliberate or accidental, and check your own behavior to ensure that you aren't inadvertently withholding or distorting evidence for others. Strong personal beliefs have a way of altering perspective.

Trust but Verify

This phrase was popularized by President Reagan during a time when the Berlin Wall fell and the Iron Curtain was removed. It implies that we should give the benefit of the doubt, but also doubt some of the benefits we're hearing.

In business and personal dealings, we're apt to trust *without question* those who are closer to us and those who have a track record of success:

- Family
- Trusted subordinates and aides
- Respected experts and authorities
- Those who others we trust in turn trust

The problem with these *automatic* trust sources is that when they let us down it's more than a disappointment, it's a catastrophe. We all have felt the devastation of a child who has lied in critical circumstances, or the accountant who embezzled funds from an account we never thought we had to audit, or a doctor who didn't pay close enough attention and prescribed the wrong course of action.

There is a continuum for trust that might look like the following:

Paranoia	Suspicion	Benefit of the doubt	Trust	Trust but verify	Blind faith

Both extremes are dangerous in daily dealings (we're exempting religious beliefs; however, the great preponderance of clergy we've interviewed has stated that doubt is a key element of faith). We subscribe to the notion that *the absence of evidence is not evidence of absence.* And Woody Allen wryly commented that "Just because you're paranoid doesn't mean that no one is following you."

Profitable Language

Ask *yourself* whether what you're been told can be easily verified if it has a major impact on your business and life.

Suspicion is best left to detectives and benefit of the doubt to those who have consistently performed up to expectations and beyond. But the difference between trust and trust but verify is immense.

Thousands of institutional and private investors trusted people who trusted Bernie Madoff and his hidden Ponzi scheme investment strategy. The returns were absurd, but the very people who were screaming to recover their funds after the fraud was exposed were the same ones in the private clubs in Palm Beach screaming that he accept them as investors. They verified nothing.

In fact, the federal oversight agencies verified nothing. They had been suspicious of Madoff's operation, but never delved into his actual accounts, accepting instead false summaries and obfuscation. Most of the media were the same way, writing *exposés* only after the house of cards collapsed publicly.

Trust lost is harder to recover than gaining trust in the first place. When someone has lied or fudged the facts or even passed along bad information they thought was correct, they usually sacrifice all future credibility. While we tend to be forgiving and rehabilitate public figures (politicians, athletes, entertainers, and so on), even that isn't always the case. Lance Armstrong, who lied for years about his illegal *doping* regimen to win cycling tournaments, isn't about to be the spokesperson for any major product or cause. Tiger Woods was not only reviled after his scandalous womanizing became known, but his golf game also collapsed, and while once considered the person to overtake Jack Nicklaus's major victories, he now seems as if he will never win another.

The Catholic Church lost millions of its faithful and tens of millions of dollars when the ultimate bastion of trust—priests and the hierarchy of prelates—was embroiled with pedophilia and cover-ups. (And consider this: Less than 5 percent of the Catholic clergy was ultimately involved, which is a smaller percentage than public school teachers found guilty of child pornography and pedophilia.)

This is why we favor *trust but verify* on our continuum for major issues (and, perhaps, even minor ones). The following is some language to consider to employ this tactic:

- How can I easily verify whether I'm hearing facts or opinion? What is the source? What is the evidence? What is the observed behavior?

  Note that, increasingly, we see an insidious admixture of *fact* and opinion in the newspapers, on talk radio, and on television. People with their own agenda peddle facts which suit them but do not suit empirical reality.

- What are the chances that a sincere source has, himself or herself, blindly trusted others? Am I watching a *herd* movement, a surrender to normative pressure? Am I being asked to *be one of the in crowd* without sufficient analysis of the crowd's motive or direction?

  There is huge, unprecedented normative pressure delivered on social media platforms, from YouTube to Facebook, Twitter to LinkedIn, and the yearning for conformance leads to the viral extension not only of unsupported positions but even of pure myth. You can constantly find advertisements posing as a third-party *opinion* on these platforms.

- Am I viewing the mixed media effect? Is a trusted expert providing *expertise* in another area, using his or her repute but not factual support?

  Marshall McLuhan first reported this in his seminal work *Understanding Media* and his phrase *the medium is the message*. (He anticipated the world wide web by 30 years.) We have a tendency to attribute expertise in *all fields* to those who actually excel in one field. Hence, the reaction to singer Barbra Streisand's strident political commentaries by her critics with *shut up and sing*.

I've been involved in projects where I simply assume what the next step is, but when it goes wrong and I turn to the next page on the instructions, I find that I assumed incorrectly. I hadn't verified my own belief. This doesn't matter so much when you can pull apart some boards or rewire a lamp, but it matters a great deal when you might choose the wrong college, new car, or investment vehicle.

Have you ever gone on a vacation based on brochures, or web video tours, or even the recommendations from people you don't know well? Quite often, this doesn't turn out well. That's partly because any property will put its best face on, including airbrushing that face or even lying about it. But it's also because people whose taste you're unfamiliar with may love rustic while you love luxury, or you may have a different idea of *luxury*. I've gone to restaurants people have raved about where I've realized the recommenders have actually never tasted food that I'd consider excellent.

Beachfront can be 20 yards or two blocks. You need to verify the distance. *Thousands of happy guests* can overlook tens of thousands of unhappy guests (this kind of subterfuge is common in book reviews— *Grossly unfunny* is reprinted simply as *funny*).

In an Internet age, you can usually find a surfeit of reviews to help you verify products and services. But the best solution is the same you should use for literary critics: Find a couple with whom you constantly agree *or disagree* and use them as a barometer, following the former and ignoring the latter.

Let's look more closely now at the tactics for critical questioning.

CHAPTER 4

Critical Questioning Skills

The essentials of interrogative language: We deal here with the fundamental management issues (past, present, and future) and how to apply logical inquiry, relevant questions, and rapid validation to improve efficacy and create commitment rather than mere compliance. This is language at work to improve job performance.

Solving Problems

Problem solving is often done extremely poorly (trial and error) or extremely ineffectively (statistical analyses complete with fish bones). So let's establish the language of the criteria and of the resolution.

A problem has three criteria for it to be a legitimate problem in our language:*

1. There is a deviation of actual performance (or a person, process, or piece of equipment) from the expected performance.
2. The cause of the deviation is unknown.
3. We care.

You can see this illustrated in Figure 4.1. The objective of problem solving is to find the cause of the problem and to remove it because, otherwise, we are simply adapting to its effects. The cause is always rooted in some change because if nothing changed, the performance would have continued without deviating.

---

* The people who popularized the approaches in this chapter are Chuck Kepner and Ben Tregoe in their classic work, *The Rational Manager*, McGraw-Hill. These precepts were also used by the British Army in WW I and by the ancient Greeks.

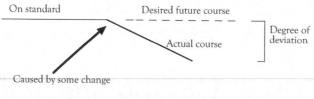

Condition:
1. Deviation of actual from desired course.
2. Cause is unknown.
3. Deviation is serious enough to concern us.

Figure 4.1 The anatomy of a true problem

Finally, we have to care. A lamp might be making a humming sound that is barely audible and we don't know why, fulfilling the first two criteria, but it doesn't matter and so we don't have a problem, merely a humming lamp.

The questions to ask, therefore, are:

1. Do we have a deviation of actual from expectation, and, if so, what is it? This can be misleading, in that if three people complain about their common supervisor, the deviation is the complaints, not the supervisor at this point. You can see the power of the correct language. Finding out *why* they are complaining (cause) will determine if the supervisor is indeed at fault or if the complainers are taking out some other grievance on their boss.

2. Do we know cause? This, too, can be highly ambiguous if we're not careful. We "jump to cause" every day by assuming we know the cause, or finding blame, or simply guessing. We say, "Oh, it's the sales people again," or "Here's what happened last time," or "What do you expect from a rookie?" But cause must be verified. Of course, if we *do* know cause, then we no longer have a problem, but rather a decision to make (which we'll cover in the next section).

3. Do we care? Can we live with it or not? Is it a *necessary evil?* I'd choose not to live with a leak in the ceiling, I'd want to find the cause. But I can live with a TV remote that has a two-second delay in changing channels. I don't know why it does it, it's not supposed to, but fixing it is more trouble than it's worth.

You can see in the diagram that some change had to have occurred at or prior to the deviation taking place. We call this *relevant change* because any change taking place post-problem solving is often needlessly delayed, because too many changes are considered.

Profitable Language

Think and say *cause* not *blame*. Problem solving is the search for cause that will remove problems, not a hunt for scapegoats.

How do we find relevant change? We look for distinctions around the deviation.

What:

- What is the object or person with the deviation, and what or who might it be but is not?
- What is the deviation, and what might it be but is not?

Where:

- Where is the deviation occurring geographically, and where might it occur but is not?
- Where is the deviation relatively, and where might it be but is not?

When:

- When in clock or calendar time did the deviation first occur, and when could it have but did not?
- When in the life cycle of the object or career did it occur, and when could it have occurred but did not?

Degree:

- What is the scope of the deviation, and what could it be but is not?
- Is the deviation growing, declining, or stable?

Obviously, we adjust these questions relative to machines, processes, and people, but you get the idea. We're trying to find the *distinction* about the deviation itself, and then ask what relevant changes could have affected those distinctions.

Example

A sales person is successful selling all products but one. The distinction is that one product was most recently introduced. Another distinction is that the normal trainer was on vacation, and this one person's training was done by another sales person.

The distinction is the single product, since all other products were included in prior training. The relevant change was using another sales person, not accustomed to training, to fill in for the trainer.

To remove and correct the cause: Provide remedial training with the proper trainer.

Note that you can correct a problem by finding cause and removing it, or choose to live with a problem by adapting to its effects. Fixing a hole in the roof removes the leak, putting a bucket under the leak saves the carpeting even though the leak still exists.

All of this involves choice, which brings us to decision making.

Making Decisions

We can enter the decision-making process in one of two ways: As a result of a problem, we now must make a decision about the best way to remove it (corrective action) or to live with it (adaptive action). Or, we may realize that we must make a decision about something and enter decision making directly.

The definition of a decision is this: making a choice among options. It is a *present* dynamic. Problems have already occurred, they are past-oriented. But decisions are made in the present.

Decisions involve three elements:

1. Objectives: What are we trying to achieve and what are we trying to conserve (investment)? Ideally, we want the greatest result with the least investment, known as return on investment (ROI) in both our business and personal lives.

2. Alternatives: What are my options for reaching the objectives? These are various courses of action available to me.

3. Risk: What peril or danger, from minor to major, does each course of action potentially present, and how can I prevent the occurrence or minimize the impact?

Profitable Language

Most people most of the time either ignore or automatically minimize risk because they are so thrilled with the potential benefits. The grass may look greener, but not if there is quicksand underneath.

Let's examine what we might call a decision-making funnel, seen in Figure 4.2 below, which represents the proper sequence of action in decision making and examine the proper language along the way.

A decision statement creates the expected outcome, with subject and verb, noun and action: To buy a new car, to choose a vacation destination,

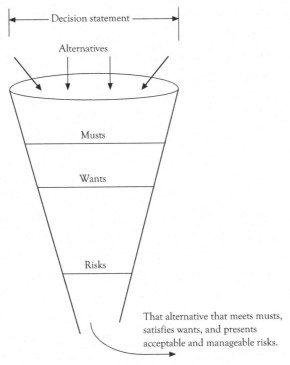

Figure 4.2 The decision funnel

to select a college. Note the language: These are not *binary* choices (do it or don't do it). These allow for a range of options, as opposed to, "Should we go to the mountains?"

Based upon the nature of the decision statement, we generate alternatives (beach, mountains, Europe, *staycation*, and so forth). These can originate in our experience, research, friends and colleagues, creativity, and so on. The alternatives are then compared against the objectives, which should be viewed in two dimensions.

Musts are needs critical to the decision. They are reasonable, measurable, and mandatory. For example, if you're looking for a new car, and can finance only $45,000, then the *must* is "maximum cost of $45,000." If you ignore that, there's a name for it: bankruptcy. A *must* meets all three of the criteria or it's not a must. In that case it's a *want*.

A *want* is an objective that's desirable, not mandatory. You may want the car as soon as possible, so that if it's on the lot and doesn't have to be ordered, it's more desirable. But if the car on the lot is more than $45,000, you can wait for a less expensive one.

As you can see in the funnel, alternatives generated by the decision statement are rejected if they fail to meet the musts, and if they perform poorly against your wants. (A car available in a week is superior to a car available in two months if they are both less than $45,000.) The funnel is a culling process.

Finally, we have risk, which is too often overlooked or given short shrift. *Every* alternative has some risk, and we can examine risk the following way:

- Probability: What is the probability of the occurrence? (Poor weather in the rainy season in the Caribbean is very high.)
- Seriousness: What is the nature of the impact on us if the occurrence can't be prevented? (It generally rains in the early morning and the weather is clear by midmorning.)

We try to prevent the probability factor through avoidance actions and we try to mitigate the seriousness factor through mitigating actions.

Ultimately, we want the most highly beneficial alternative *but within acceptable risk levels.* Some of us (and some entire industries) have higher risk tolerance than others. The critical factor is to assess the risk relative to the benefits *before* committing to a decision.

Note that you usually enter the decision-making chain after some decisions have already been made. For example, to buy a new car implies that you need transportation, you need to buy not lease, and it will be new, not used. To choose a vacation site implies that you've chosen to take a vacation and have dates in mind.

To *raise* the level of decision, to find strategic levels in business, ask "Why?" That drives you up the chain to more general decisions. To *lower* the level in the chain, ask "*How,*" which gets you to more tactical questions: What kind of sport utility vehicle or what color? What vacation resort on St. Bart or what kind of accommodations?

The language of decision making, therefore, must take into account all three components (objectives, alternatives, risks) and act as a culling device, not an additive device to enable you to hone in on the best alternative within acceptable risk. It's a very easy dynamic, but often completely ignored in personal and business decisions because the wrong language is employed (e.g., Should we expand into Europe? Is Syracuse a good school?).

Once we make effective decisions, we have to protect them.

Planning

Once we've made some decisions, we need to plan for success.* We've solved problems arising in the past, made decisions in the present, and now must implement and protect our decisions in the future. It's no accident that our three primary actions relate to past, present, and future.

The language of planning looks like the following:

1. What is the plan?
   For example: To purchase new computers

---

* This is the true meaning of *planning,* to move something forward from the present into the future. *Strategy,* on the other hand, is the creation of a desired future state and working backward to today to make it happen. Planning is an extrapolation, strategy is exponential.

2. What are the major steps in the plan?
For example:

- To seek referrals from trusted others.
- To select the supplier.
- To negotiate the purchase and price.
- To install the equipment.
- To train the users.

3. What are the truly critical steps or highest priorities?
For example: To install the equipment.

4. What are the potential problems in this step?
For example:

- Disruption to existing business.
- Failure of new equipment when we go *live*.

5. What are the likely causes of that problem?

- Disruption to existing business:
  o Failure to run dual systems to take care of existing customers during transition.
  o Lack of space and overcrowding.

6. What are preventive actions for the likely causes?

- Failure to run dual systems:
  o Plan continuance of current system and switch to new system overnight, not during business hours.
  o Train existing personnel using overtime, not during regular shifts.

7. What are contingent actions if problem occurs and cannot be prevented?

- Disruption to existing business:
  o Have team in place to notify all existing customers of the short-term disruption.
  o Offer any customers experiencing problems a free month of service.

We talked in decision making about risk, and risk having two components: probability and seriousness. The planning process is one of examining a plan to isolate the major steps, then choose any of particular critical nature (e.g., a failure in that area would doom the endeavor), and then attempt to both reduce probability of risk and mitigate effects of risk.

If you ask the average person what they would do if building a structure and worried about fire, they would usually respond with fire sprinklers, fire extinguishers, escape doors, insurance, and so forth. Yet all of these are contingent actions, *only effective to some degree after the fire has started.*

Preventive actions would include posting "no smoking" signs, separating combustible materials, ensuring correct electrical wiring, and so forth. We rightly honor firefighters for risking their lives rushing into burning buildings, but it's the fire marshals and the permit process that are important in preventing the fire and the danger. The best sprinkler system in the world requires a fire to prove its worth.

Profitable Language

Effective preventive action saves time, lives, money, injury, and embarrassment.

Our language has to reflect these key distinctions because like cause and effect in problem solving, or objectives and alternatives in decision making, we often blur the line between preventive and contingent action in general. Insurance is nice, but it prevents nothing, only ameliorates the suffering and loss to some degree.

Since contingent actions are mostly unused except in the case of failed preventive actions, we require monitoring to ensure their ongoing effectiveness. A great many home fire extinguishers have failed to work precisely when needed because their pressure had drained and no one had bothered to check the gauges. (A deicing machine purchased for a southern airport where ice was rare was finally called into action and promptly broke down because no one had bothered to continue to service it.)

Elevators have inspections for their brakes, sprinkler systems are evaluated for pressure, insurance policies require premiums be paid. All such actions ensure that your contingencies are not only present but *will be effective if called upon.* Preventive actions must also be inspected regularly. Are the "no smoking" signs still posted? Have you ever seen an important highway sign with directions or warnings overgrown by vegetation? No one is monitoring the preventive actions.

If we look at both problem solving and planning, we can see quite simply the relationship of issue to action in Figure 4.3. All concern cause and effect, and past or future.

If you want to remove cause in the past (problem solving), you must take corrective action. But if you choose to live with deleterious effects, then you are taking adaptive action. If you want to prevent cause in the future, you must implement preventive actions, but if you seek to mitigate future effects you are planning contingent action.

It's really that simple. But your language and intent have to be clear. We've all been at a meeting where this conversation takes place:

Person 1: We have a big problem here.
Person 2: I agree, our department will allocate resources to this decision.
Person 3: Very good, let's protect this plan.

As you've seen, problems solving, decision making, and planning have very different starting points (find cause, choose an alternative, protect a plan), and these three people are walking away from their meeting

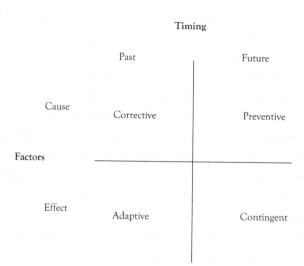

Figure 4.3 Actions available

theoretically in concert but actually starting at vastly differing points. It's no wonder that so many meetings result in no effective actions.

The language is all wrong.

It's wise to forget the *old* management language of *organizing, managing, and planning* and start to think of and speak in terms of *past, present, and future*. Too many problems aren't solved because people are making decisions without knowing cause (or having found *blame*) and too many plans are defective because people haven't identified risk and its components.

Innovation

Our final major action is innovation, what Joseph Schumpter called *creative destruction* and what I call *applied creativity*. There are many good ideas in organizations, among entrepreneurs, and from think tanks and R&D units—but very few of them ever reach the market in terms of a viable, profitable, product or service.

Whereas problem solving seeks to restore performance to a past level of performance, which we *know* can be met (after all, we have a deviation *from* that level of performance), innovation seeks to *raise* the level of performance to a new, improved standard. Call it a *positive deviation,* and you can see where language, once again, becomes vital in providing direction.

Our experience is overwhelming in that unless there is a concerted focus on innovation as a separate and valued discipline, it simply does not happen with any regularity.

Profitable Language

Innovation changes the risk–reward ratio from decision making in that greater risk in vital for greater reward.

The visible depiction of innovation looks like the following:

Note that there's a danger of the situation *deteriorating* if the innovative plans don't work (more on that to follow), but also that even if the new standard of performance isn't met, there may well still be improvement.

If you reconsider the chart in Figure 4.3, and our use of planning process to ensure success, the innovative actions would look like the following:

1. Potential Innovation

   • Advertisers place their own ads in the publication.

2. Likely Cause

   • We provide software for major browsers.
   • We reduce ad prices when self-placed.

3. Promoting Actions

   • We reduce ad prices when self-placed:
     ○ We survey advertisers and ask at what price point they would take the time to place their own ads.

4. Exploiting Actions

   • Advertisers place their own ads:
     ○ We heighten sales efforts to bring on new business.
     ○ We use advertisers who agree to self-place as testimonials for new business.

You can see in this example that we seek to promote the likely causes of our innovations (promoting actions), which are analogous to preventive

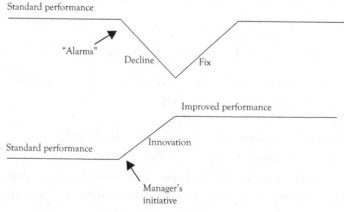

Figure 4.4 Problem Solving vs. Innovation

actions, and we create exploiting actions to build on the improvement, which are analogous to contingent actions.

Innovation is a discipline that requires the proper language to direct people to the right ends and sustain the initiative. In most organizations it is inappropriately assigned to a *special unit* (e.g., a *skunk works*) or a designated time frame (a *retreat*), or to special people (R&D). Hence, the need to distinguish it from creativity, and even more so from problem solving, decision making, and/or planning.

Before leaving this chapter on critical questioning skills related to the past, present, and future, we'd like to provide some guidelines in both professional and personal matters.

Guidelines for Effective Critical Questioning Skills

1. First, identify your starting point.

    Ask whether you are trying to solve a problem, make a decision, plan, or innovate. Remember, you're *never* doing more than one of them at any one time with any one issue.

2. Ensure that all stakeholders are in agreement.

    Ask whether everyone is in concert and agrees with the starting point. Establish the definitions in this chapter if it helps. Never assume that everyone is in agreement just because they seem to be. Find out if the language *and* the meaning of the language is consistent.

3. Don't confuse cause and effect.

    An effect is something that impacts you adversely (in problem solving), but it always has a cause. Understand that if you're merely addressing the effect (adaptive action), you have chosen to live with the problem.

4. Don't confuse cause with *blame*.

    If your language is organized to find culpability or scapegoats, you won't necessarily find cause, and taking punitive action against individuals seldom removes the problem. For example, changing an account manager doesn't remove the cause, which may be lack of authority granted to frontline people.

5. Recognize that risk has both probability and seriousness, which need to be separately considered. Learn to ask *not* what the danger is, but what the probability and seriousness of the danger are.

6. Distinguish between the need for both preventive and contingent actions, and the primacy of preventive action to save money, time, injury, and embarrassment. Fire extinguishers will not prevent a fire.

7. Make innovation a part of your vernacular, with the intent of consciously and deliberately improving standards.

CHAPTER 5

Critical Situation Skills

Personalized business language: We follow up in this chapter with specific and singular needs of business interactions, which can be addressed rapidly and "on the fly," if one masters the underlying use of information-to-knowledge transformational language.

Resolving Conflict

Conflict is seldom based on factual information that is *right or wrong*. More often than not, it is (by dictionary definition): *an incompatibility between two or more opinions, principles, or interests.* Different perspectives, perceptions, and experiences contribute to potential conflict in any situation. These differences can be related to:

- Values and beliefs
- Goals and responsibilities
- Resources
- Processes and procedures
- Individual differences and styles
- Imbalance within a team (relationships, communications, leadership)

Even though conflict frequently has a negative connotation, it can be highly positive. Just as Schumpeter called innovation *creative destruction*, conflict creates *healthy tension*, wherein people act with transparency and not hidden agendas.

When these differences are viewed as assets (instead of road blocks and distractors), they help pave the way to consensus, creativity, and commitment. (Consensus is something one can live with, not have to die for.)

When approached and handled effectively, conflict can be a significant catalyst in successful planning, execution, implementation, problem solving, decision making, and innovating. In essence, it's a necessity for successful outcomes in any organization. A conflict, in and of its self, is not destructive. *It's the lack of effective conflict resolution* (along with conflict avoidance) that causes impasses and destructive downward spirals.

If these differences (conflicts) are a good thing, then resolving conflict is more than fast-tracking (or demanding) others to *see it my way*. The key to dealing with conflict is *not* your ability to merely influence or convince others by what you tell them (or demand of them). It begins with your ability (and intent) to, first and foremost, understand others. The route to understanding is (once again, our reoccurring theme) *asking the right questions at the right time*. (When I was young and managing international sales forces, my idea of conflict resolution was to *shoot* everyone in the room and be the sole survivor. I learned there were always larger guns.)

Here are the keys to creating successful conflict resolution:

1. Focus on the process, the issue, the problem, the decision …not the person(s). Don't find blame or assign fault or culpability.
2. Seek to understand first, not argue … ask the right questions.
3. Listen for understanding and with acknowledgment. Be empathetic. (Empathy: recognizing and understanding what the other feels, not sympathy, which is feeling what the other feels.)
4. Focus on the favorable outcomes, benefits, and value related to the mission, vision, strategy, stakeholders, and desired results.

Keep in mind, these keys are applicable whether you are facilitating conflict resolution with others or you are directly involved in the conflict.

Profitable Language

Conflict is *seldom* a problem with *chemistry*. It's more often a case of honest disagreement about objectives (where are we going) or alternatives (how will we get there).

Let's look at each of these key steps in more detail:

1. *Focus on the process, the issue, the problem, the decision, not the person(s).* Don't expect to change others' core beliefs or behavioral styles. Don't be critical of the person's personality or preferences. Don't cite blame or fault. Avoid blanket statements such as "You always ..." or "You never ... " Instead, focus on and deal with the specific matter at hand.

2. *Seek to understand ... ask the right questions.* In order to resolve anything, you must be aware of others' positions first. Ask questions to seek out the *who, what, when, where, why* of the situation. Ask additional probing questions as needed to determine the root of the conflict, not just the symptoms or effects. This is not meant to be an interrogation, but an exploratory conversation. This positions you to have a full understanding before attempting to be understood.

3. *Listen for understanding and with acknowledgment. Be empathetic.* Do you listen for understanding? Or, do you listen in order to respond? Listening is a science. Listening for understanding is an art. We've all been taught to keep quiet while the other person is speaking. But, here's what hasn't been taught: the technique of confirmation, which not only cites what the other person is saying, but also, more importantly, demonstrates your understanding. (What is said and what you understand aren't always one and the same!) If you were to exactly repeat the words said, that would only confirm you heard what was said. It's important to paraphrase and summarize what you've heard (put it in your own words) to confirm or validate your understanding. If there's a disconnect or misunderstanding, this gives the other person the opportunity to clarify. (Note: This technique does not suggest agreement. It's merely a path to true and accurate understanding.)

    The skill and value of *empathy* can easily be an entire chapter (or an entire book) all on its own. (Google *empathy* and you'll find 32,500,000 results.) So, let's discuss empathy here in context of conflict resolution, and to do that, let's look at the working definitions of what empathy *is not* and what it *is*.

Contrary to popular belief, empathy is not *walking a mile in their shoes*. It is not *having been there and done that*. It is not *being able to fully relate to what the other person has experienced*. In the purest sense, empathy is recognizing what the other person is experiencing or feeling. The formula for acknowledging empathy is to state: "*It seems as though you are feeling* (fill in the blank with the feeling/emotion)."

Acknowledging someone's feelings relative to the situation (happy, satisfied, elated, sad, confused, scared, frustrated, angry, disappointed, and so forth) provides a sense and reassurance of understanding. If you don't pinpoint the emotion or feeling correctly, usually the other person will appropriately clarify or correct you, which is exactly what you want. Example:

- *You*: "It seems as though you are frustrated with the new procedures."
- *Them*: Yes, I am frustrated.

or

- *Them*: I'm not frustrated, I'm angry that the procedures changed again and we weren't consulted first.

With either reply, the result is that both of you can confirm the feelings.

Being empathetic is not meant to be agreement or approval. Instead (and more importantly), it is an acknowledgment of understanding, which is key to conflict resolution.

4. *Focus on the favorable outcomes, benefits, and value related to the mission, vision, strategy, stakeholders, and desired outcomes.* Often, conflict is around differences in input or principles, not necessarily around desired outcomes that may very well be mutually agreeable to all parties. Once you know and understand the source of the conflict, you can focus on and position what's best in regard to achieving the desired results.

Conflict resolution isn't about compromise or demands. It's about questioning, listening, understanding, and confirming, and, ultimately, it's about influencing others to see things from a perspective that can still be in their best interest.

Negotiating

Negotiating is the process of reaching agreement with two or more parties. It's the give and take, win–win, win–lose, *or lose–lose* proposition. The focus on the process and end result of negotiating is different from traditional conflict resolution, and, yet, the same communications skills apply—questioning, listening, understanding, confirming, and empathy. When it comes to negotiations, it's important to know *how* your audience thinks, not just *what* they think or how they feel.

Negotiating also requires a different level of rapport, persuasion, and confidence. If you're in a position of power over your audience, it's easy to insist and declare what the final agreement will be. However, the savvy negotiator uses personal power (influence and persuasion) instead of positional power to create the win–win.

Techniques to utilize when negotiating are as follows:

- Listen to the needs and wants of the other party.
- Ask noninflammatory questions to gather additional information and understanding (not "How did you end up in

---

Case Study

Years ago, Mercedes-Benz negotiated a *merger* with Chrysler. A new car even emerged from it, the Crossfire. The Crossfire looked very nice, but it was underpowered and under-performed, and it is no more.

Nor is that merger.

Subsequent evaluation of Mercedes executive strategy shows that the negotiation wasn't conducted in the best of faith. What Mercedes called a *merger* was actually treated as an acquisition, as evidenced by the quick and encouraged departure of most of the senior executives at Chrysler shortly after the takeover.

Negotiations have to take place in the best interests of both parties, otherwise they aren't truly negotiations, but rather muted hostilities.*

---

* One of my political science professors told me once that "Warfare is simply the least subtle form of communication."

this pickle?" but "What would you like to accomplish from here?").

- Identify common elements of both sides.
- Identify disparities of both sides.
- Emphasize the positive and agreeable aspects of your proposal and theirs.
- Tactfully challenge other's views, without intimidating.
- Effectively handle objections to your proposal or position without being defensive.
- Identify top priorities and deal breakers—yours and theirs.

The process of effective negotiations is more about well-honed communications skills and interpersonal skills versus the actual content of the negotiations. It's having the right level of emotion, without exhibiting or promoting destructive emotion. It focuses on consummate questioning and listening techniques, not threatening power plays. It's the competency of *taking inventory* (deal breakers, priorities, needs, and wants) throughout the discussion, as these can easily morph or they can abruptly and drastically change.

Profitable Language

Every decision has a business and a personal component. Logic makes people think. Emotion makes people act. Successful negotiations involve business and personal components. It appeals to both logic and emotion.

The most effective tactics for negotiation:

If we revisit decision making for a moment, we see the need for *musts* and *wants*. A *must* is something critical and mandatory (and measurable), without which you will fail. A *want* is merely a desire, though some wants are more desirable than others.

Applied to negotiations, *never sacrifice a must for a want*. In chess, you don't take a knight if it means losing your queen. In business, you don't accept a cosmetic improvement in return for losing productivity and performance. Whether negotiating with unions, investors, lawyers, suppliers, or customers, never make that trade.

The vaunted Ritz-Carlton Hotel approach at one point had all employees capable of offering up to $2,500 in free amenities to please an unhappy guest—when, in fact, often a mere *thank you* or free drink would have sufficed. Nordstrom's one-time policy of accepting *all* returns— even if perspiration stained, damaged, or not from their store—gained publicity but also red ink, since it enabled transgressions and the wrong kind of customers.

These are negotiation tactics that sacrificed musts (profit) for wants (please every customer, reputation as a *good* company).

Case Study

When I moved to San Francisco, the realtor showed us homes all day long. I had said that air conditioning was a must, since I have allergies. She had said that one doesn't need air conditioning in the Bay Area, but I told her that I did.

She showed us home after home without air conditioning, but would say, "We're close to the school," or "Look at that view," or "Resale values here are going to be excellent." She wanted me to trade off my must for wants I hadn't even requested.

We fired her.

Most people think that negotiation is about win–lose, a zero-sum game. It's not. It's about win–win, where we're both happy, even if not ideally happy. But bear in mind, the opposite of win–win is *lose–lose*.

Both Mercedes and Chrysler took a bath because of poor-faith negotiations. Mercedes should have been more honest and Chrysler should have been more diligent.

How about you?

Exploiting Success

Do these questions for a postproject debrief (the infamous postmortem) sound familiar:

- What didn't meet expectations and why?
- How can we prevent that from occurring again?
- What do we need to do differently next time?
- What constraints or barriers did we face?
- What hindered your progress?

- How can we do better next time?
- Who blew it?
- How do we recover from this (or hide it)?

Even if you add a first question on *success* (as many debriefs do), most of the discussion focuses on what didn't go well. While those discussions have a time and place, how often do you and your team discuss the intimate details of success in order to exploit that success? We're not referencing the cursory celebration party. Instead, we're suggesting a postmortem on *success* factors. This will position you and your organization to exploit the current success and create repeatable successes. (Novel idea, huh?)

Profitable Language

It's better to know *why* you're good than *that* you're good if you want to replicate success.

Here are additional ideas on exploiting success at different levels of the organization.

Exploiting Individual Success

Implement a routinely scheduled one-on-one meeting with managers and direct reports. The format of this meeting is not designed to be a mini-performance review. Instead, it focuses on three areas:

- Accomplishments (results)
- Game Plan (objectives, action items, priorities)
- Open Forum (ideas, suggestions, concerns, Q&A, FYIs)

This is the *employee's meeting*. The manager may facilitate it, but the idea is for the employee to come to the meeting to discuss things from his/her perspective. The meeting is designed to be casual, informal, and conversational. As the employee discusses accomplishments, this is the manager's opportunity to recognize and acknowledge these successes. The accomplishments don't have to be big, bell-ringing, life-saving, heroic measures. It's the employee identifying *what* they did, *how* they did it, and *why* that accomplishment or result is of VALUE. The value can focus on or be beneficial to any or all of these areas:

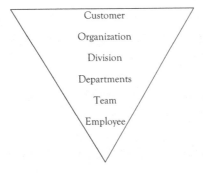

The value can also be aligned with areas such as mission, vision, strategy, revenue, profit, customer loyalty, company culture, quality, streamlined processes and procedures, and so forth.

This discussion positions the manager to explore and acknowledge employee accomplishments, in essence, to exploit successes. And, you don't have to throw a parade to do so.

This may sound like an elementary activity. And, yet, executives throughout a variety of organizations have told me how this tool and process have drastically changed and improved communications throughout their organizations.

NOTE: If you are interested in more information about this process, check out the Appendix. (Everything you ever wanted to know about effective one-on-one meetings is there!)

In the same way, you should debrief and celebrate the success of any initiative or project, and you should also debrief and celebrate your own incremental successes. Leaders can be successful and have no idea how or why. In order to exploit success (repeat it), you must be able to *identify* the components of it.

Unconscious
Competence

Conscious
Competence

Conscious
Incompetence

Unconscious
Incompetence

The foregoing progression demonstrates that we are normally at our best in *unconscious competence* (we tie our shoe without thinking about it, do our job without thinking about it, and so on), *but we can only learn and improve in conscious competence* (making a loop in the lace to tie the shoe, creating certain computer responses to do our job, and so on).

Here's a quick example: Fold your arms and then your hands very fast three times. We'll wait.

Now, try it again with the opposite arm on top and opposite thumb on top. You can do it, but only after some brief difficulty, until you return to conscious competence from unconscious competence.*

Examining victories requires the conscious competence of what we did to improve and succeed, and what needs to be incorporated in every future, similar scenario. That's why golfers need swing coaches and actors need directors.

---

* We always put the same arm or thumb on top throughout our lives, we never change, just as a given rattlesnake will always coil either clockwise or counterclockwise, but will not alternate.

CHAPTER 6

Critical Results Language

Language on the front lines: Since results, not actions, are the key, these are some specific techniques to apply at "mission critical" juncture points. There are relatively few key judgment areas where a slight difference in the language of inquiry and validity can create a huge impact.

Asking for the Sale

Assumptions, without validation and confirmation, can be the Achilles Heel of success. We think they understand. We think they agree and are aligned with the game plan. We believe we're on the proverbial *same page*. And, then, their actions (or lack of) totally surprise us. You're thinking, "Hey, what just happened here? We discussed this and now they are disregarding what we agreed on." However, in reality, was there truly *agreement*? Did you ask for confirmation?

We've all experienced this scenario. It's frustrating and disillusioning for all parties involved. If you could revisit the conversation, you'll most likely discover that you never *asked for the sale* (to calibrate interest and degree of agreement), and you never truly *closed the sale* (confirmed agreement). Not asking for the sale is like running the entire race and stopping short by failing to run through the tape.

In a traditional sales environment, not asking for the sale with prospects and customers is thought to be a fear of:

- Rejection and being told no
- Having to deal with difficult objections
- Feeling awkward, uncomfortable, pushy

However, not asking for the sale is seldom fear. It's significantly more basic and less emotional. It's not being aware of the value and necessity of the technique in everyday communications. Asking for the sale is not a slick sales move. It's a savvy communications skill. Everyone should be proficient (unconsciously competent) in this technique. To gain this level of competence, it's important to know the *value* of asking for the sale in order to know *when* and *how* to use it in your role as a leader in conversations you have on a daily basis:

> *Value*: The implicit becomes explicit. The value of asking for the sale is to eliminate any assumptions or ambiguity regarding agreement or disagreement (lack of buy-in). It's the equivalent of the *handshake agreement* where all parties are in agreement.*
>
> *When*: Asking for the sale begins as a progressive process throughout the conversion and culminates with asking your audience a direct question at the right time. This is done to elicit a *yes, no, or maybe* in agreement to move forward. Throughout the conversation, you are conscious of and recognize areas of agreement (alignment) as well as areas of disagreement or objections (possible roadblocks to be addressed and overcome). When the time is right, you avoid assuming your audience is aligned with you and you actually *ask* for that confirmation to validate your assumptions.
>
> *How*: Create *touch points* along the way and throughout the conversation. Listen and probe for understanding, acknowledgment, agreement, disagreement, and concerns. When *all stones have been turned* (you've answered questions and overcome objections), it's as simple as asking some version of: "Is there anything else we need to discuss in order for you to move forward?" If the response is *no* (which, in fact, is a positive at this point), then it's time to run through the tape! Go for it by *asking for the sale*. Now is the time to make the implicit explicit. Confirm with some version of, "Great, then you're ready to ―――――――――?"

On the other hand, if the response to your question ("Is there anything else we need to discuss…") is *yes* (which means you haven't yet closed the sale), continue the discussion to determine if:

---

* *Instantiation* is the act of making the intangible and abstract tangible and practical.

- You need to provide additional information.
- There are objections cited that have not been overcome.
- There are additional objections and concerns that have not been surfaced or voiced.

Profitable Language

We often make an early *sale to ourselves* by kidding or deluding ourselves about the progress we've made.

Sometimes, you think you've *turned over every stone*. But, in fact, you may have misinterpreted the situation. The following are some common scenarios that can create a false sense of agreement prior to asking for the sale:

- *"Do you understand?"* Even when the answer is *yes*, never assume *understanding* means agreement. Your audience may understand perfectly, but not necessarily agree.
- *"Does this make sense?"* Just because it *makes sense* doesn't mean you have agreement.
- *"Do you have any questions?"* The absence of questions does not denote agreement.
- *Failing to recognize an objection as an objection.* Not all questions are objections. Questions merely need to be answered. Objections (which can be in the form of a statement or a question) are based on some element of dis-agreement or concern. If the objection is of high priority for your audience, it needs to be overcome. High priority objec-tions that are not overcome can prevent agreement. (We'll talk more about overcoming objections later in this chapter.)

Some are great at asking for the sale, but don't recognize when they've gained commitment and *closed the sale*. Therefore, they keep talking and keep talking and run the risk of eventually losing that sale and commitment!

There's an old sales training story about a sales person debriefing with the sales manager who was along on the sales call. The conversation goes like this:

Salesperson: "I don't understand. She seemed so interested. I thought for sure I was going to close that business."

Manager: You did close the business.

Salesperson: I don't understand …

Manager: The customer agreed to buy and you took it back when you continued to talk and explain. Then, it happened again. The customer agreed a second time, and again you kept talking. Finally, the customer gave up. You sold it twice and then went on to lose it twice. That's why you didn't get the sale. You have to know when to ask for the sale, when you've closed the deal, and when to stop talking or selling.

Asking for the sale and closing the deal in daily conversation isn't selling a product or a service. It's the culmination of effectively positioning, influencing, and confirming—which is the epitome of sales in any situation. It's the art of gaining commitment instead of demanding compliance.

Case Study

I was visited at my office in San Francisco by a representative of the Chamber of Commerce. I said within two minutes, "It's a must for us, see my secretary to get a check." The rep kept talking, pointing out membership benefits and the backgrounds of other members.

Finally, after 10 minutes, I said, "Go get your check now, or keep telling me about the chamber and we won't join." After an uncomprehending stare, the rep vanished on the verge of grabbing defeat from the jaws of victory.

Gaining Support and Exerting Influence

"Command and control. Dictate and demand. Rank and rule." Short of the military, these leadership styles have gone by way of *servant leadership* and sweat lodges in their effectiveness in today's organizations. (The only reason I didn't state they've gone by the way of the dinosaur is because, unfortunately, those styles aren't yet completely extinct!) I'm not suggesting that leading should be decision by committee or that holacracy is the way to go. What we are emphasizing is the fact that leaders in today's world must be able to gain support and influence others, day in and day out, in a variety of situations.

Continually.

I've worked with a myriad of leaders throughout a variety of organizations (the entire scope of public, private, profit, not-for-profit, small business, large business, family business, local, domestic, global, and so forth). Through the years, I have unscientifically categorized leaders as:

1. Leaders who were *liked* personally and socially, but not necessarily respected as business leaders.
2. Leaders who weren't particularly liked (personally or socially), but were respected and applauded for their business approach and leadership style.
3. Leaders who were relatable and respected. (Being *liked* was irrelevant in this category.)

My unscientific observations focused on which leaders were the most successful in gaining voluntary support and influencing others—internally and externally. Interestingly, the leaders in the third category were *the star leaders*. The second category leaders were next in line. And, sadly, those who were the most liked and the least respected (first category) may have had a lot of friends in the workplace, but they were lacking in their ability to gain support and influence for results. They were found lacking as successful leaders.

Profitable Language

Engaging and partnering is far more effective in influence than orders and punishment.

What constitutes relatable and respected? Here are the characteristics regarding gaining support and influencing others:

- They don't use position power (acquired authority) or their personal power (credibility and influence) exclusively. They know when to use which, as there is a time for each. (Position power is about policy or discipline. Personal power is about persuasion and influence.)

- They not only walk the talk (lead by example), they consistently talk the walk (lead by consistent and proactive messaging).
- They know how to ask the right questions at the right time (relevant to the matter at hand).
- They don't view challenging questions, objections, or resistance from others as being undermining or uncooperative. They realize the value of these conversations and engagements.
- They know how to answers questions, overcome objections, ask for the sale, and close the sale.
- They clearly and succinctly communicate the *what, how,* and the *why* of *value* of any significant decision or initiative. They can easily customize this for any given audience—including providing the answer to the ever popular question from their audience of "What's In It For Me?" (Even when this question isn't verbalized, it's always on someone's mind, so the effective leader knows to address it whether it's asked or not.)
- They position things to be relevant and meaningful for others. They communicate and frame the alignment of decisions, efforts, and action with mission, vision, strategy, and ethics. They don't leave the interpretation of that connection to chance. They actually connect the dots with and for others.
- They are appropriately empathetic.
- They engage others effectively.
- They control without being controlling.
- They know how to successfully negotiate.
- They never pretend to have all the answers all the time.
- They display confidence and instill confidence in others.
- They create avenues for voluntary commitment versus expectations of mandated compliance.

If this list sounds familiar, it's because we've already presented every one of the characteristic in some context. The fact is *all* of these characteristics are essential to gaining support and influencing others. If you ignore, eliminate, or violate any one of them, you exponentially diminish your ability to be successful in this regard.

Overcoming Rejection and Objection

What would a scripted courtroom scene be without an attorney dramatically jumping out of the chair and vehemently shouting, "Objection your Honor, I object!!!"?

In a courtroom, an objection is raised after the opposing attorney asks a question, during testimony, or while evidence is being introduced. An attorney voicing an objection is similar to stating, "Foul, offsides, or out of bounds" in hopes the judge will agree and sustain the objection. If sustained, the judge disallows the testimony, the question, or the evidence. If the judge overrules the objection, then the testimony proceeds as is and the objection is no longer relevant.

Courtrooms aside, objections in every day conversation take on a different flavor.

- Objections can be in the form of a question or a statement. Don't confuse a simple inquiry for additional information with an objection that needs to be effectively addressed and overcome. "I disagree with your premise" is an objection. At face value, "What is the basis for that conclusion?" is merely a question.
- Objections are seldom clearly announced as objections. Short of someone blatantly stating they disagree, objections may be subtler. They can be extremely subdued. They can even go completely unstated. Nonverbal behavior often indicates objection, for example, when eye contact is lost or eyebrows are raised.
- In a courtroom, the judge gets to state to the jury, "You will disregard that information." In your world (and in the legal one, let's not kid ourselves), that bell can't be unrung. Unlike a switch you turn with an adverse reaction and quickly turn it back again, you can't take back your words.

- You're on your own. There's no judge calling the shots as to what's admissible and what's not. Lawyers who don't have the merits of a case use the law. You have no such option.

And, last but not least, the most significant distinction is:

- In the context of conversational language (such as *selling* an idea or decision, negotiations, resolving conflict, gaining support, influencing others, innovation, strategic planning, and change management—all the other areas we discuss in this book), an objection is a sign of *interest*. It's not an attempt to shut down the conversation, as it is in a courtroom. It means your audience is at least interested enough to continue the discussion and to further explore. Even if they are discussing what appear to be roadblocks, they are giving you the opportunity to address their concerns. Objections are a sign that your audience is not indifferent. Objections are a good thing. You just need to be comfortable and prepared to handle them.

Profitable Language

An objection is valuable; apathy or indifference is a killer.

There are two ways to deal with objections:

1. Preventive: Anticipate and respond to the expected objection before it's stated. This is the preemptive approach. "What will they say to try to prevent this idea being accepted? What's in their own interest that might be antithetical to this idea?"
2. Contingent: Wait for the objection(s) to arise and then deal with them. "Let me respond to each of your three objections right now." "Why do you feel that way when you've never mentioned that factor before?"

To maximize success, use both techniques. You don't want to be exclusively preventive. Don't attempt to proactively address each and every objection that could possibly be cited. There may be common objections you can anticipate and address as you present information. However, because objections are truly a sign of interest, *individual objections help you recognize where one's concerns and interest might lie, which provides great insight in the process.*

Here's a step-by-step approach to dealing with objections:

1. *Listen and recognize*: As we've mentioned, it's ineffective and unproductive to treat a simple question or comment as an objection when it's not one. Just address the question or comment and confirm with your audience that they are satisfied with the information you've provided. On the other hand, if it's truly an objection, then move to the next step.

2. *Discovery*: This is not the time to become defensive and launch into a rebuttal. (That is, don't treat an objection as rejection.) Instead, *be curious*. Ask additional questions for clarification. It's important you know and fully understand the objection before addressing it. Ask the right questions and then paraphrase your understanding to minimize the opportunity for misunderstanding. Sample questions include:

   • *Tell me more about that …*
   • *Help me understand how this affects …*
   • *Is this a significant concern for you?*

3. *Acknowledge and respond*: Once you have an understanding of the objection and its scope, acknowledge the objection and respond appropriately. (Depending on the type of objection, this may be the perfect time to be empathetic.)
   Your response may be to:

   • Offer additional or clarifying information
   • Cite a similar situation and the positive results
   • Focus on the value to your audience
   • Provide a contrarian position (offer a different point of view for consideration without it being a defensive rebuttal).

4. *Confirm and Gain Commitment*: After step 3, ask, "Have I answered your concern(s)?" If they agree, move to step 5. If not, continue to discuss as needed.

Note: Some objections may be smoke screens—they are minor objections (or distractions) that aren't the heart of the concern or the issue at hand. This is why you want to make sure you surface any true objections that can be deal breakers. A key question to ask is, "If it weren't for this (objection or concern), would you be willing to do XYZ?" And remember, as with negotiating, there are some objections that are not deal breakers (meaning, they may or may not be voiced, but they will not prevent *closing the deal*). This is the difference between *musts* (deal breakers) and *wants* (desires) we discussed earlier in decision making.

5. *Ask for the "sale"*: As we mentioned earlier in this chapter, never leave it to chance as to whether your audience is in agreement with you. You *must* ask for the sale to confirm commitment. If they don't agree, either you weren't successful in step 3 or they may have additional objections or concerns that still need to be addressed. Provided they agree, move to step 6.

6. *Close the sale—Run through the tape:* you haven't succeeded until the contract is signed, agreement is obtained, hands are shaken, and so forth. Pour cement on the confirmation.

Now, let's look at a different angle related to objections. Let's talk about the most effective way to state an objection when someone else is taking the initiative in the conversation with you:

1. Don't be coy and don't use smoke screens.
2. State where you see the value, benefits, or positives.
3. State any objections or concerns clearly.

This formula eliminates uncertainty and puts the cards on the table. If the other person isn't forthcoming in the information you need to make a decision, then go after that information and ask the right questions.

Case Study

While meeting with the division president, we were discussing the leadership strengths of a particular executive who was a top team member reporting to the president. The president acknowledged,

"When Dave has an idea or makes a suggestion, by the time the conversation is over, you're not only onboard, you honestly believe it's also your idea. It's not coercion or manipulation, or some form of bait and switch. He's an expert at presenting the info and engaging you in the conversation. He asks the right questions, addresses any objections, and focuses on the value related to our strategy. And, it doesn't matter who he's talking with. He creates a partnership, not just a win–lose proposition. He's a master at influence and gaining support."

Resilience

"The thrill of victory and the agony of defeat … "

This became the well-known line in the opening scene of ABC's *Wild World of Sports*. The show captured the highlights of sports competitions around the globe. While the show was about sports, that very line became a common catchphrase for grandstanding the winners and the losers (successes and failures) in any situation. We've all been there, on either side of the equation at some time or another. Not just in sports competitions, but in daily life.

With an intentional focus on your success (the thrill of victory), we've spanned a wide spectrum of circumstances in this book that you regularly face. We have:

- Presented the value of asking questions (versus merely telling, directing, and demanding).
- Explored how to move from data to wisdom.
- Provided insight and steps on how to effectively utilize critical questioning skills, critical situation skills, and critical results language.
- Encouraged you to debrief and celebrate collective and individual successes, including your own.

Now, at this point, the question is, how do you deal with the absence of success? When all does not go well or when the desired results are not achieved, how do you remain resilient and continue to move forward? How do you recover from the *agony of defeat?*

We all experience moments (or what sometimes feels like trends) of less than desirable results, missing the mark, or outright failure. No matter how experienced, talented, and skilled we may be, we all have situations and circumstances where we need to deal with difficult and less than ideal outcomes. We all have situations and circumstances where we need to be resilient in order to be truly successful.

In some cases, the agony of defeat is collective (the opposite of collective successes), and you need to create a sense of collective resilience within a team or the organization overall.

In other cases, it's *up close and personal*. It's your ineffectiveness, misstep, or failure, and you need to focus on your own resilience.

Resilience is the capacity to recover quickly from adverse situations with little or no residual damage or lingering effects. It is psychological elasticity.

The following are keys to resilience:

Bouncing back from defeat: Like anything in life, defeat can be minor, major, or anything in between. Bouncing back isn't related to the degree of defeat. It's directly related to how you view the adversity and how you leverage it. Abraham Lincoln lost most of his early elections, Steve Jobs nearly lost (and did lose) his own company, athletes return to start the day after losing the game for the team, and so on.

Learning from setback: Hindsight in any situation can be 20/20. It doesn't predict future success, but it does allow you to deconstruct what worked and what didn't. Look for cause and effect, as well as patterns, trends, and one-offs in the situation. Analyze how these contributed to the past situation and what you may need to add, change, or delete for a similar future scenario. West Point cadets study defeats, not merely victories, to learn what to avoid in the future.

Stress as a positive not only a negative: Is your glass half empty or half full? Are you a pessimist or an optimist? Is your self-talk negative or positive? Your answers to these questions may determine whether you use stress as a positive catalyst or if it handicaps and undermines your ability to be resilient. Stress can motivate some while it hamstrings others. It can be an energy booster or an energy drainer. If stress is chronic or you feel that it's *imposed* on you, chances are it will have a negative effect on you. On the other hand, if you feel in control (even in the face of failure or defeat), stress can be a great motivator. Believe it or not, well-managed stress can make you more resilient in any circumstance. Eustress is the *positive stress* that creates the adrenalin rush prompting great work under pressure and deadlines.

Remaining optimistic: This tip is based on the premise that you are optimistic to start out and that you can maintain that optimism through the good times and the not-so-good times. Dr. Martin Seligman at the University of Pennsylvania is the rock star of positive psychology, and his book, *Learned Optimism*, details how one's self-talk can improve behaviors, habits, and influence.

Absorbing setback without assigning it to poor self-worth: Resilient leaders can separate setback, failure, and defeat from their own self-worth. They are not one in the same any more than your successes make up your self-worth. This doesn't suggest they refuse to take responsibility for their actions or decisions. Instead, it means they have the confidence to not let success or failure define their self-worth.

Maintaining identity despite outcomes: Your self-worth is independent of your efficacy. That is, you are not as good as your last victory or as poor as your last defeat. Your self-worth should be constant, so that you can accommodate victory without becoming egocentric and absorb defeat without becoming depressed, as you can see in Figure 6.1.

Self-esteem as a roller coaster

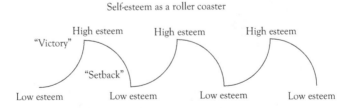

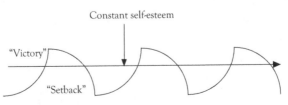

Figure 6.1 Constant esteem

Being Wisely Resilient

I spent (wasted?) a lot of time and effort trying to fix a failing situation I was directly involved in. (I'm talking years!) At the time, my self-talk repeatedly nagged me with common phrases such as "hang in there, don't give up, you can do this, take responsibility, don't abandon the situation, don't be a quitter, you're smart enough to fix this, to make this work and have it be successful." In response to my self-talk, I continued ad nauseam (and quite unsuccessfully) to attempt to influence to a positive outcome.

Being wisely resilient means recognizing when something *can't be fixed* and it's time to face it and deal with it. Whether it be relationships, jobs, projects, or new initiatives, in these cases, *giving up* isn't the failure. The failure is continuing an unproductive situation that has no hope of being successful short term or long term.

Does self-talk promote you or hinder you in being wisely resilient? It's well worth exploring with your own self-talk.

CHAPTER 7

Overcoming Language Pressure Anxiety

Language in the breech: Some of the otherwise best and brightest are great in rehearsal but fall apart on the front lines. We address here how to proactively take control of key influence and persuasion language so as to create a "martial arts" of verbal communication.

Managing the Media

Even steeled and feared CEOs sometimes unravel in the face of media inquiry. So do presidential press secretaries. In fact, so do Presidents. (Remember Bill Clinton's syntactically dreadful "It depends what 'is' is?") Bold military leaders, athletes who perform under pressure, celebrities accustomed to the spotlight, all have withered before media heat.

Yet, this is an age where there is no expectation of privacy any more. Anything we say, write, or portray may well be used against us, not in a court of law, but in the court of public opinion.

Whether it's the 2015 Super Bowl champion New England Patriots and deflated footballs or it is presidential hopeful Hillary Clinton declaring that she and Bill were *dirt poor* when they left the White House, the media gives airing to these bloopers, but the speakers are the ones committing them.

And, if it occurs to people like that, what about you and me?

Now, you may be thinking, "I don't interact with the media. No one is trying to interview me." But we need to adjust the scale and adjust to current times.

The *media* today include Facebook, YouTube, LinkedIn, Twitter, and any number of other social platforms. The media include things you create in writing, such as résumés (which sometimes contain unexpunged white lies that return to ruin a career). Brian Williams, the NBC anchor, was removed from the most popular evening newscast on television for exaggerations and lies that were pointless, but which he repeated so often that he probably came to believe.

The point is that the media are all around us. Supposedly, there are apps that allow your message or photo to automatically be erased within a short time, but there are no other apps created to reverse that ability! Histories on computers are not eliminated simply by choosing to do so on the computer menu, nor are cell phone histories.

Profitable Language

Ask yourself if what you're considering saying, writing, or depicting will stand you in good stead under other circumstances, including merely the passage of time.

Here are some rules for dealing with the media, whether the communication is instigated by media sources, third parties on the media, or you:

1. Always consider that you never know who will read something. Business careers have been subverted and job openings lost because a superior or interviewer took the time to find the other person on Facebook. Some one recently applied to me for coaching, but I refused him when I learned on Twitter that he prided himself on being a hacker—which is illegal.
2. Attack or debate positions not people. *Ad hominem* approaches are not only damaging to your own reputation but can engender long-term animosities. What we once called *word-of-mouth* and now call *viral marketing* can work two ways, and when respected peers say someone is treacherous, others will not go near them.
3. Practice and proof read. Forget about typos and be more concerned with the nature and character of your communication. There is no such thing as *withdrawing an e-mail* any more than there is such a thing as the jury disregarding a toxic accusation. Don't use examples from companies that aren't in the public domain (e.g., printed in the media) without permission.

4. Never assume your words are ephemeral. Someone is *always* recording. Just as a secret never remains a secret if more than one person knows, there will be someone making notes, recording on a device, or taping no matter what your remonstrance against it. I see people in Broadway theaters doing this all the time, despite the risk of being tossed out of a $300 seat.

5. Review upside and downside. You should be communicating with language that provides you with a 90 percent upside and only 10 percent downside (i.e., benefit vs. risk). Don't tell people you guarantee your plan will work. Tell them it's the best plan available and has the best chance of working.

One of the very best practices with the media is to use metaphor in place of pedestrian words. Move into the high-speed lane. We'll cover that later below. But first, let's look at profitable language in debate.

Determined Debate

A debate, by common definition, is a formal exchange of ideas where opposing views are discussed. When you think of a formal debate (political, public forum, student debate teams), there are extremely strict rules to be followed. There are affirmative positions and negative positions, or *point or counterpoint* discussions. Each side has a designated time frame to present, to refute, and to overcome objections. The debate is moderated and judged. A winner is objectively declared either by a scoring system or subjectively by an often infamous public opinion polling system.

As we all know, this is not how it works in the everyday debates you engage in as a leader. Yet, some of the same core foundations for formal debate apply in your world:

1. Be well informed: Understand your position and the counter position (the *thesis* and *antithesis*).

2. State your position and a short summary or description that supports your position. Even though your position may appeal to emotion, there must be logic in the foundation.

3. Respond to and overcome objections.

4. Confirm agreement or ultimately agree to disagree (strive for *synthesis*).

Recognize that an effective debate is not a series of "Yeah, but" monologues by each person. It must be an integrated, push-and-pull conversation.

Academic debaters (college and high school debate teams) are required to debate the position assigned to them. They don't get to choose whether they agree or disagree with the premise. They are expected to debate and defend accordingly. They practice in mock debates. This mental agility builds a skill set not many are exposed to in real life, such as:

Looking intently at each side of a position
Creating "pros and cons" for each side
Anticipating points of agreement and disagreement
Designing the logic of overcoming objections
Utilizing effective verbal and nonverbal cues

We can all benefit from what these students master as the foundation of effective debate.

Profitable Language

Curiosity doesn't kill cats, it improves their ability to hunt and escape peril. The same holds in debate.

In my first decade of *adulthood*, I was convinced that if your opinion was different from mine, then I was right and you were wrong. And I was more than happy to debate you while professing and insisting on the merits of my *rightness*. In my second decade, under the same circumstances, I still thought I was right and you were wrong. The difference was I didn't necessarily have to tell you that you were wrong and I certainly didn't need to initiate or engage in a debate. I was OK with just knowing I was right. In my third decade, I finally evolved to realize that in matters of opinion, perception, and interpretation (versus hard core facts), it's not a matter of right or wrong. It's merely a matter of different. Different didn't equate to being right (good) or wrong (bad). Different just equaled different.

This very revelation changed the way I engaged with others. In the face of debate (or even casual conversation), I no longer led with being insistent, adamant, and unrelenting. Instead, I first became *curious*. As a master of heated debate (from 0 to 60 in mere seconds), I stepped back and became *curious, exploratory, and inquisitive*. I started asking questions instead of making bold, determined statements. (Instead of declaring, "People don't respond well to merely being paid more if there's not recognition," I asked, "In what ways will money, by itself and without recognition, improve morale?" And, I asked with the appropriate tone of curiosity instead of one of self-righteousness!)

Being curious and inquisitive in this sense doesn't mean you should become a timid soul with no opinion and then recoil at the very thought of debate. It means that if you understand the *what, how, and why* of your position *and* of the other person's position, you pave the way for the following to surface:

1. You may or may not gain new insight that influences your own opinion or perspective. But, either way, it's worth exploring.
2. You may find that you have more agreement and common ground than you expected or realized (such as you may have agreement on expected outcomes, but not on execution, or vice versa).
3. You better understand the other person's perspective, and this best positions you to make your case (influence others).

In our discussion on negotiations (Chapter 5), we are explicit that the goal is to create a win–win outcome, not win–lose or lose–lose. A similar goal is true with debate. You want to create a win–win even in the midst of a polarized debate. It shouldn't be a *zero-sum game*, where another's losses create your gain. That is ultimately a lose–lose proposition.

How does the effectiveness and finesse of debate come into play in business versus social situations? The key distinguishing factors include:

- You will have to continue to work with these people and *play nice* in the future.

- You may not *own* the decision in any case, but merely be a stakeholder or advisor.
- Even when unequivocally correct, you don't want to embarrass or hurt anyone because others may be intimidated by your actions in the future (or seek retribution).
- If you're in a genuine team environment, everyone wins or loses together, so trying to *win* a debate at someone else's expense ultimately hurts you anyway.
- Leadership qualities are usually evaluated based on gaining consensus and commitment and not by body count on the roadside.

No one can *win-win them all*. How do you know "when to hold them and when to fold them?" We're not talking about bluffing, as in a card game. Instead it's recognizing:

- You know you have a great hand and you're going *all in*. You're confident you can influence others.
- You appear to have a playable hand, but you're not sure how it compares. This will make you tentative in presenting your position. (Revisit steps 1 to 4 discussed earlier.)
- You realize don't have a great hand. Your position isn't as strong or worthy as you thought it was coming into the debate. By asking questions and understanding the other person's position, you voluntarily alter your position. Don't view that as losing or being defeated. You are ultimately still creating the win–win.

As in all such vital interactions, the language you choose will make the difference.

The Metaphoric Question

Metaphor: A figure of speech in which a word or phrase is applied to an object or action to which it is not literally applicable.

"If a picture is worth a thousand words, then a metaphor is worth a thousand pictures." A metaphor paints a picture and tells a story by using a few key descriptive words in one short sentence. Metaphors are a *figure of speech*. They're not merely a literary technique used solely by creative writers, poets, or novelists. They are a powerful tool to incorporate into your everyday communications.

Why use metaphors? What's the value for you and your audience? Metaphors uniquely position you to:

- Engage and intrigue your audience.
- Use figurative language to express literal meaning.
- Speak *visually* by creating vivid images for your audience to see things from a new perspective.
- Make the unfamiliar familiar.
- Make the controversial more palatable.
- Make the complex simple to understand.
- *Fast-track* your audience's comprehension.
- Turn *boring verbiage* into significant messaging.
- Create messaging that is more personable, memorable, and powerfully persuasive for your audience.

In essence, metaphors are the secret decoder ring in communications. They let your audience easily decipher your message. One of my favorite metaphors is *the oxygen mask imperative*. Airlines tell millions of people daily to put their own oxygen masks on first before trying to help others. In other words, you have to help yourself first. The same applies to personal health, well-being, safety, and success.

The following are other examples of common metaphors related to the mind and memory:

- Her mind is a *steel trap*. Absolutely nothing escapes.
- His brain is a *sieve*, allowing the smallest particles of pertinent information to seep out.

In each of these examples, the person's mind is figuratively described as something it cannot be literally (*steel trap, sieve, oxygen mask*).

This figurative descriptor *paints the picture* of the meaning for your audience.

Simile: A figure of speech involving the comparison of one thing with another thing of a different kind, used to make a description more emphatic or vivid.

Simile is a type of metaphor, as it's also a figure of speech using comparisons. Where metaphor makes the direct connection (suggesting the two subjects are equal), simile is more of an associated meaning by comparing similarities. A simile makes the comparisons using the words *like* or *as* (versus a metaphor that uses *is*). Staying with our mind–brain theme, here are examples of similes:

- My brain is like the overflowing apartment of a *habitual hoarder*. It's clogged with unorganized piles of useless information that get in the way of me being able to quickly access vital information.
- His recall is *like a solid-state drive on a brand new computer*. It's instantaneous with no lag or delay.

Descriptions and comparisons stated as metaphors and similes are an essential tool in effective communications.

Idiom: A group of words established by usage as having a meaning not deducible from those of the individual words.

Idioms are another form of figure of speech known as *figurative expressions*. They are expressions used so often that they have become commonplace and are often times considered to be clichés. Because of their common use, the intended meaning is easily translated from the figurative expression. Examples of common idioms:

- *It's raining cats and dogs.* (It's raining especially hard.)
- *He has his head in the sand.* (He's not acknowledging what's happening or he's in denial.)
- *She's under the weather.* (She's not feeling well.)

- *If we play our cards right ...* (If we make the right choices ...)
- *At the end of the day ...* (Focusing on the end result ...)
- *We see eye to eye.* (We're in agreement.)
- *The difference is like night and day.* (The difference is obvious.)

Idioms in business run rampant. Because idioms are oftentimes commonly known expressions, they are no longer unique. They may not have the impact and value of *original* metaphors and similes with your audience, but this doesn't mean they shouldn't ever be used. They do have their place in language. It's merely pointing out that idioms will not have the profound effect on your audience as a well-crafted metaphor or simile.

Profitable Language

You and your point will be memorable, like familiar pieces of music one can't remove from recall—an indelible imprint—when you use metaphoric language.

Litotes: Ironical understatement in which an affirmative is expressed by the negative of its contrary.

No discussion on figurative language would be complete without referencing *litotes*. The term may not be familiar, but litotes are ubiquitous. Often recognized as a *literary double negative*, it's known as a rhetorical litotes. While double negatives can sometimes be confusing, a true litote is usually well understood. Examples of litotes:

- *It's not bad at all.*
- *You're not wrong.*
- *He's no dummy.*
- *This is no minor matter.*
- *I do not disagree.*
- *You won't be sorry.*

As you can see, litotes are intended to emphasize the actual message through the emphasis of a negative (stating what it *is not*). They catch people's attention because they may not be immediately understood. Your audience may need to take a split second or two to *decipher* the true meaning of your message.

Where it may be effective messaging, *you need to be cautious in the use of litotes.* Your message can be interpreted as downplaying a positive, as though you're not willing to give full credit where credit is due and it then comes across as a minimal or a backhanded acknowledgment. It can also be misinterpreted as being inappropriately sarcastic. So, use your litotes wisely. (*She's not a bad leader* may not be one you want to use.)

When it comes to figurative language, the great thing about creating metaphors and similes is, short of following the appropriate structure, there's no *right or wrong* to formulating a metaphoric statement. Here are your practice steps:

1. Select your subject or object, the essence of your message.
2. Brainstorm and identify the characteristics of your subject.
3. Look all around you (literally and figuratively!). What resonates with the characteristics of your subject?
4. Use the following format:
   Metaphor: X is a ...
   Simile: X is like ...

To show that there can be a variety of comparatives for the same subject, consider the following examples:

1. Our sales performance is like a pendulum constantly swinging back and forth from peak performance, through downturns, and back up again. (Simile)
2. This year's sales growth has been like riding a rocket shot into space. (Simile)
3. The current sales cycle is a roller coaster in action. As we expected, it's been up, down, fast, slow. It's been fun and it's been scary. (Metaphor)
4. Last year, our sales team was not only on the super highway, but they were also in the fast lane going at maximum speed while avoiding all delays and detours. (Metaphor)

Tip: Use the essence of metaphoric language in formal presentations. For presentations using visuals (such as PowerPoint, Keynote, or handouts), use pictures to capture and reinforce the essence of your metaphoric message and *talk to* the relevance of that picture. We're not talking about traditional (and often times boring) spreadsheet and pie chart-type visuals. Instead, for our four examples above, show and speak to a picture of a pendulum, a rocket, a roller coaster, or the fast lane of a super highway, all of which are more effective and longer lasting than the ad nauseam bulleted items of verbiage on page after page after page.

Creating Your Own Reality

Perception is reality.
There are things known and there are things unknown, and in between are the doors of perception.

—Aldous Huxley

The eye sees only what the mind is prepared to comprehend.
—Robertson Davies, *Tempest-Tost*

In Chapter 3, we explored perceptions, honesty, truth, and empirical evidence. Ideally, in your role as a leader, you seek empirical evidence to determine *truth*. However, you are interacting in the world around you where people operate under the fundamental premise of *my perception is my reality*. What they hear and see is filtered through their own values, beliefs, and experiences, which then creates their own version of their truth (their perception).

To that point, your role is to also influence those very perceptions. Often, it's up to you to actually *distort* others' perceptions of reality in order for all to be successful. (Keeping in mind, of course, that your mission to distort reality is for good, not for evil!)

Steve Jobs was well known as the genius and master of this influence, which is known as the *Reality Distortion Field* (RDF). If RDF sounds like something from Star Trek, it's because that's exactly where it originated. In the original pilot episode, aliens use the RDF to *create their own new world through sheer mental force.*

There are many stories as to how Jobs *acquired* RDF (the skill set and the label). However, those who were in his immediate atmosphere of influence are consistent in their views of his mastery of the concept and the power of it. These quotes, from those who worked closely with and knew Jobs well, best describe his ability to create reality distortion (quotes from *Steve Jobs* by Walter Isaacson, 2011):

- "In his presence, reality is malleable. He can convince anyone of practically anything. It wears off when he's not around, but it makes it hard to have realistic schedules."* (Bud Tribble, credited with *labeling* Jobs with RDF in 1981)
- "If you trust him, you can do things." "If he's decided that something should happen, then he's just going to make it happen." "And the effect was contagious." (Elizabeth Holmes)
- "The reality distortion field was empowering. It's enabled Jobs to inspire his team to change the course of computer history with a fraction of the resources of Xerox or IBM. It was a self-fulfilling distortion. You did the impossible, because you didn't realize it was impossible."(Debi Coleman)
- "The reality distortion field was a confounding mélange of a charismatic rhetorical style, indomitable will, and eagerness to bend any fact to fit the purpose at hand." (Andy Hertzfeld)

In Jobs' own words, he identified with a line from Lewis Carroll's *Through the Looking Glass*, in which he related to RDF. After Alice laments that no matter how hard she tries she can't believe in impossible things, the White Queen retorts "Why, sometimes I've believed as many as six impossible things before breakfast."

Not all is positive with reality distortion. The other side of coin includes these drawbacks of reality distortion as utilized by Jobs:

- What he says today may not be what he says tomorrow. He was famous for changing his mind without warning.
- He was known for disagreeing with someone's idea today and coming back at a later time and posing it as *his new great idea.*
- After adamantly disagreeing, he would suddenly (without warning) agree and adopt that very position as his own, without explicitly acknowledging his change of mind.
- He believed himself to be infallible.

---

* All quotes listed here are from Steve Jobs by Walter Isaacson, 2011.

Jobs was known for behavior of extreme polarities. Some may say this behavior had nothing to do with reality distortion, it was just Jobs's personality. But, in fact, the polarities are extremes of the good, the bad, and the ugly of reality distortion.

The *reality* is … reality distortion can be a double-edged sword. How do you maximize the positive effects and minimize the negative effects?

- *See the possibility in the impossible.* As a visionary and strategic thinker, you must *see* what's feasible beyond what others see as the *impossible.* Realize that you should be working with a telescope, not a microscope.
- *Be realistic in your distortion.* It's not a matter of creating artificial expectations just to get people to work harder, faster, and more. It's creating expectations that others can actually reach, even though they may not see or realize that at the time.
- *Believe what you profess.* You can't disrupt reality if you are viewed as the *talking head,* merely being the good soldier and carrying out the orders and directives of someone else. People will perceive you are not truly on board and that perception will be their reality.
- *Be a constant and consistent force in creating the new reality.* The less present you are, the more the motivating impact of reality distortion wears off or fades (as noted in the preceding quotes about Jobs). You can't afford to drive a future stake in the ground and expect everyone to successfully get there on their own. Remember, even if they trust you, they will not have the certainty you have.
- *Provide people the resources to do the impossible.* Don't expect people to *believe and rise to the occasion* if they don't have access to the right tools and resources to be successful.
- *Create incremental successes.* Do your part to monitor and audit progress toward result at a level appropriate to your role as a leader.
- *Hold everyone (including yourself) accountable.* Stay on a *success path.* Celebrate progress and implement real-time path corrections when needed.

The magic of reality distortion is this: When individuals and teams successfully achieve what they thought was impossible, they have a new perception of reality. They may never proactively see the same reality you see as early as you see it. But, they learn to appreciate your ability as a visionary and strategic leader. They start to believe and trust that with your leadership the impossible can be possible.

Profitable Language

Behavior is influenced by perception, and perceptions are conveyed through your language.

Create your language with the idea in mind of influencing others toward *your* intended reality, not some fait accompli left by others' perceptions. As examples of reality distortion, good and bad, bear in mind these hyped and incredibly repeated phrases that influence the behavior of voters, legislators, members, donors, media representatives, investors, and similar key stakeholders:

- War on women
- Weapons of mass destruction
- Kardashians
- Paying forward
- Date rape
- Just say no
- War on drugs
- Quarterly profits
- Eco-terrorism
- Climate deniers
- Crowd sourcing

You get the idea. Powerful people create powerful distortion fields in their favor.

CHAPTER 8

There Are a Few Good Questions, a Lot of Good Answers

Language fine-tuning: These are advanced techniques and nuances to increase speed and ease of gaining facts and honest analysis. They allow for flexibility and adaptation outside of one's "home turf" and with a wide variety of people not generally under one's control.

Adjusting Language to Audience

One size does not fit all.
In the days of domineering, autocratic, bureaucratic management, the leader's style ruled all. That individual style was a constant that was *imposed* on others. There was little, if any, consideration in adapting one's management or leadership style. Orders were barked out and everyone was expected to *fall in line and follow suit*. This was true figuratively and often times literally. While this style was prevalent in organizations in days gone by, it still exists. (Think of the military as an extreme example of this.)

Steve Jobs might be considered a *my way or the highway* type of leader. Bill Belichick of the New England Patriots is that kind of football coach.

The other extreme is the leader style that is nurturing, encompassing, fully embracing and operates exclusively in a world of decision by committee. These leaders want everyone to be *happy*. They figuratively lead via a fireside chat while creating a *kumbaya moment*. They hire consultants who lead retreats to camp in jungles or build sand castles on beaches.

To be successful in today's organizations, leaders can no longer impose their preferred style on others and be universally effective for the long term. This is particularly true in the language they use. Even with language, *one size does not fit all* applies.

You cannot merely exhibit your preferred style of static language with no adjustment. Successful leaders adjust and adapt language based on audience, circumstances, purpose, and perception. Successful leaders know how to position and pivot accordingly, in any given aspect of language and communications.

Leaders are most likely to be cognizant of adjusting language to the audience. But, many are not aware of the necessity and value of adjusting language for circumstance, purpose, or perception. After all, we've all been taught to *be consistent* in our messaging. The key is to be consistent in messaging, while appropriately adjusting language. The information here applies whether:

- Your audience is individual, small group, large group, or a global reach
- The setting is casual or formal in nature
- Your medium is face-to-face, audio, video, or print
- Your communication is strategically planned, ad hoc, or spontaneous

Let's explore adjusting language in each of these situations:

Adjusting Language to Your "Audience"

Think of the audiences you communicate with on a regular or periodic basis:

- Executive committee or council
- Peers
- Direct reports
- Teams, departments, divisions, companywide
- Clients or customers
- Prospects
- Shareholders or stockholders
- Board of directors

- Advisory board
- Partners, vendors, suppliers
- Regulators
- Associations
- Media
- Community
- Public at large

In consideration of your various audiences (individual conversations and group conversations), our advice is not to *dumb-down or elevate* your language based on your audience. It's a matter of *strategically focusing your messaging in regard to positioning content and language that is appropriate to you audience.*

- *What* is to be communicated (topic, issue, concern, announcement, game plan, recovery, and so on).
- *How* and *why* is this topic relevant to this particular audience? Be *explicit* not *implicit*. While this particular topic may be universal (you are discussing with multiple audiences), the language of *how* and *why* will vary from audience to audience.
- Incorporate *examples* that are specific to your specific audience. It's imperative that you use examples that each audience can relate to versus using generic examples that every audience should be able to relate to. This means you need to change or customize examples for different audiences. Your core messaging may be similar, but your examples may be drastically different in order to drive your message.

Adjusting Language to Circumstance

What are the circumstances requiring and prompting your communications? The answer to that question determines your language. Your communications may be based on:

- Strategic direction
- Successes

- Failures
- Performance or results updates
- Proactive promotion
- Damage control
- Crisis management
- Restructure or reorganization
- Mergers and acquisitions
- New product or service announcement
- Community support or affiliation
- Competitive information
- Annual report
- Awards and acknowledgments
- Business setting and social setting

You may be dealing with the same audience in different circumstances. You may be dealing with different audiences in different circumstances. Each of these scenarios warrants an adjustment in language.

We've usually heard a significant other at home say suddenly, "You know, you're not in the office now!" That's our cue to remember that the circumstances have changed. We speak with some clients with great familiarity, but to prospects with more *arm-distance* formality. I react very poorly to a company employee where I'm doing business who meets me for the first time and immediately uses my first name. I'm neither old-fashioned nor arrogant—I'm a pragmatic business person and first impressions are lasting ones. The fact that you call colleagues or even long-time clients by a first name doesn't mean you should do that to new people under different circumstances.

The managers and captains in our favorite restaurants, our drivers, and others always use honorifics with customers: Dr., Mr., Ms. They know the circumstances merit it.

We usually have a great many clients with whom we are familiar, and well-liked and trusted. We also have many prospects who know little about us and have no experience with us. We can't expect the familiarity of the former to travel to the latter through osmosis. We have to adjust our approaches to suit the circumstance.

Some examples:

- You need to create trust with new people.
- You need to slow your language in new circumstances.
- You can't use past references and past metaphors with new relationships.
- You need to be careful with humorous, satirical, and ironic language. "How did that work out for you?" or "What made you decide to do that?" can be an innocent inquiry or a venomous question.

A brief digression, but also relevant: This is why first dates are so terror-laden and often failures. The circumstances are attended by confusing and conflicting factors: Do I appear desperate? Am I asking enough questions? Should I talk less? Can I have a second drink? Should I mention my religion? Should I mention that I have a child? Should I mention that I like their cologne?

We can all adapt that to an initial sales meeting, a college interview, a traffic officer's stop, or a pushy salesperson. We're not *ourselves* because of the circumstances, and we have to adjust.

Similarly, some circumstances create overwhelming language, intimate language, revealing language. No, I'm not talking about a beautiful moon and romantic music. I've found that bartenders seem to encourage customer revelation; people who are allowed to touch you, such as manicurists and hair dressers, engage in intimate conversations. They probably hear more honesty and detail than some therapists.

That's because the circumstances are encouraging for such talk, shared secrets with a virtual stranger. My advice is to *keep control* of your language at all times by controlling the circumstances. Just as you shouldn't get drunk or reveal secrets to a beautician, you shouldn't expect familiarity from a new prospect or immediate trust on a first date.

Adjusting Language to Purpose

You may think *purpose* is the same as *circumstance*. But, they are not the same. Circumstance is related to the condition that exists and prompts your communications. Purpose is what you want to accomplish with your communications. Continuing with our theme here, you must adjust language related to purpose. Your purpose may be to:

Inform

When you wish to inform, you should use factual language that is not mixed with opinion or speculation. *Inform* and *information* are cognates. We wish to provide facts.

Written language is an ideal medium in which to inform. There is no debate needed and interaction can be at a minimum. Questions can be asked via return mail. This is why meetings *are such poor places to exchange information and are often so boring and elongated.* Meetings are appropriate for decisions requiring consensus and joint analysis, but not for the mere conveyance of information.

You'll find many books that *confuse* opinion and fact, especially among politicians and those with philosophical agendas. One may have the opinion that vaccines are more dangerous than not vaccinating children, but that is not the scientific fact, which shows just the opposite.

Use language that is evidence and observation-based: "We witnessed lack of participation," rather than, "She is not a team player." Be succinct. Facts speak for themselves. In general, the longer one speaks or writes, the more suspect the factual nature of the communication.

The Gettysburg Address and the Preamble to the Constitution are remarkably brief documents.

Educate

This is the act of assisting in others' learning. It, too, should be factually based, except in instances of philosophic, political, or theological necessity. But we're considering it here as *social instruction.*

Educational language needs to be nonbiased and pragmatic. It should reflect a range of views and provide processes, not merely content. In other words, in today's world, one can easily look up the years of the French Revolution. But learning about its causes, aftermath, and impact elsewhere is a qualitative experience. Hence, educational language should provide insights, challenge, positive inquiry, and self-testing. It's better to ask what the years of the French Revolution were, better yet to ask its impact on America, but best of all to ask if such factors could occur again today.

In business, the question sequence would rise from, "Are we selling more than our competition?" to "Why are we selling more than our competition?" to "How can we dominate this market?"

Influence

Wielding influence means wielding language. This language anticipates or creates the self-interests of the person or group you are attempting to influence. A common example: "This offer is only good until Friday at 5 pm." The implication here is one of *scarcity*: Act now or you won't have the opportunity to act at all. You will never own this, at least not at this price.

Here is an example of language working in a group business setting. You could ask people to state what their position is on a proposed price increase. Once they state it publicly, they have committed, and it's tough (because of ego) to change their position. However, if you ask them to simply write down their position without their name and tally the responses, you can often achieve a change in opinion. (In the jury room, this is called *secret polling*, where *acquit* or *convict* can be tallied early but not with anyone committing publicly.)

Profitable Language

If you want to persuade someone to change their mind who has already committed to a position, provide *new* information (e.g., Did I mention that we would delay the announcement until after the fiscal year ends?). New information allows for a graceful change of one's mind (Oh, I didn't know that before!). Promote.

Publicize or Promote

We are allowed hyperbole when we promote:

- World's greatest
- One of a kind

- Best selling
- Most requested
- Undeniable

This is the warp and woof of the advertising industry and is generally both given and received with a grain (or a ton) of salt. The idea here is to capture attention, to use the drama of the language, and to not focus on the accuracy of the language.

We expect people to be excited by exciting language, and promotion—whether personal or organizational—must adhere to this equation. Some examples:

- The ultimate driving machine (BMW)
- Guaranteed to absolutely get there the next day (FedEx)
- Think different (Apple)
- The king of beers (Budweiser)
- Between love and madness lies obsession (Calvin Klein)
- When you care enough to send the very best (Hallmark)
- Power, beauty, and soul (Aston Martin)
- Don't leave home without it (American Express)
- It's everywhere you want to be (Visa)
- Keeps going and going and going (Energizer)
- The happiest place on earth (Disneyland)

You can *dispute* or *disprove* any of these statements, but that's not the point. This language is not about informing or educating, but about publicizing and promoting.

To summarize, here's one that I made up: If you don't blow your own horn, there isn't any music.

Dispute and Debate

When you are disputing or debating (arguing), your language must be a combination of influential and factual. What you must avoid at all costs is personal critique and attack.

The latter is known as *ad hominem* language, meaning appealing to emotions and not logic, visceral and not cognitive, subjective and not objective. Negotiation, compromise, and conflict resolution all collapse when language becomes personally offensive, employs epithets, and mocks instead of informings.

This is *schoolyard* language: "That's because you're a jerk!" But we hear milder versions of this in the boardroom, on office floor, and in e-mail. "I don't see any indication of your turning in a cost estimate" is too often met with "That's because you don't read them anyway and are too lazy to do them yourself!"

If the object of engaging in debate is to win a point or settle a dispute, then your language has to be positive. If you have ulterior motives, then your language will reflect increasingly personal and dysfunctional dynamics.

Remember: Warfare is simply the least subtle form of communications, diplomacy by lesser means.

Adjusting Language to Perception

Case Study

I was on the train to New York when the gentleman sitting on the aisle next to me left for the restroom carrying something that I paid no attention to. When he returned, he was accosted by a woman who had been sitting across the aisle.

"You have some nerve taking 10 minutes to shave in the restroom," she yelled, "it's highly inconsiderate."

"I wasn't in there for 10 minutes (he was not)," he explained calmly, "and this case has insulin, I'm diabetic, and I was taking my dose."

She left, still somewhat miffed, and I told the man I would have tossed her off the train while it was still moving. We've all engaged in these embarrassing gaffes.

Throughout this book, we've discussed the good, the bad, and the challenging of *perceptions* from multiple angles and perspectives. So, what language adjustments are required related to perceptions?

Perception, we're told, *is* reality. But whose? Only our own. Eyewitnesses often contradict each other because they have varying perceptions of the same event. "Were you watching what I was watching?" is a common query after two people have starkly differing views of the same theatrical event.

Our perceptions are altered by:

- Experiences: We tend to *categorize* or *lump* occurrences into the *drawers* and with the *labels* of past occurrences we deem similar.
- Environment: We may be distracted by noise, views, or conditions around us. In a famous experiment, a flare was lighted from a balloon high above a football game during the action, and no one reported it to authorities.
- Attention: The iconic Hawthorne Experiment, though flawed, showed that when lights were turned up, workers' performance improves, but that performance *also improved when lights were turned down.* The reason was that the perception that the altered lighting meant more attention was being paid to performance by management.
- Preoccupation: We're concerned about a family issue or a car repair or a new pet and we're distracted from the matter at hand. Others' priority is perceived by us as a minor matter or none of our concern.
- Vigilance: This sounds odd, even counterintuitive, but when we are overly disciplined and overly focused, our perceptions wane. Marshall McLuhan, of *medium is the message* fame, once observed that "The price of eternal vigilance is indifference." That's why they so frequently change the security people watching the monitors on the luggage conveyor belts. We can only pay attention for so long before our perceptions are dulled and the mango ice cream begins to taste like vanilla.
- Distraction: Have you ever missed your highway exit because you were daydreaming? Have you failed to notice that you were running out of gas? This happens in hospital operating theaters, when the wrong kidney is removed or limb amputated (this happens with frightening regularity). Perceptions in these cases have been dulled by one's habit and *unconscious competence.*

- Physicality: Not everyone has the same reflexes, hearing, sight, olfactory capability, or memory. These differences account for vastly differing perceptions (It was blue, it was green; it was six feet, it was four feet; it was 1992, it was 2002.)

Profitable Language

Never assume your perception is identical to that of others. Always test, especially in critical decisions.

How do we deal with the language of *perception reconciliation*? Fortunately, it's not difficult, at least in business settings.*

The key to adjusting language for perceptions is to test understanding. Ask the other people what they experienced. Ask them to describe it, don't merely rely on your own perceptions. Example: "I thought the client was very circumspect during the meeting, and there was no guarantee of a reorder, even the hint that we should change our sales manager. What did you think?" (Note that it's always a good idea to ask others' perceptions first, *particularly if you are their superior*, so as not to influence their perceptions!)

Test understanding with clients, customers, suppliers, regulators, peers, superiors, and subordinates. It's nonthreatening and even hard to detect what you're doing. But the language will be instrumental in alerting as to how others are viewing things, their likely course of action, how to influence them, and what to expect later.

A second major element in perception reconciliation is to simplify the issue, because of the factors above that can skew perceptions away from reality.† Ergo, we have to clarify. Examples: "If you removed the discus-

---

* In family settings, all bets are off. There is a plethora of history, emotionalism, and biases that get in the way. With family, stand fast only in principle (we have never and will never lie on our taxes) and not in taste (our first date was a movie? I guess I'm wrong, I thought it was the prom.)

† You may be wondering, "Whose reality?" For our purposes, reality is the empirical actuality that most people would find accurate, for example, the sky is blue, the sun rises in the east, most people walk upright. In business, sales are down from last year at this juncture, we've had higher attrition than industry averages this year, we're over budget for the first six months.

sion about this meeting suffering from too much noise in the halls, how do you think the client actually felt about our service?" or "If we were to assume that we all arrived here this month, what would we actually think of the operation?"

The final aspect of language in perception is to be careful of our own. We should point out what we observed or heard or sensed, but not as empirical reality and not as absolutes. We should say, "I perceived that she was rushed, and didn't want to make a hasty decision, what did you perceive?" or "I saw him keep glancing at his watch, did you see the same thing."

We need this kind of constant, mutual validations because our perceptions are often wrong. We may see someone glancing at e-mail, only to be told that person was glancing at meeting notes stored on an iPhone. I once thought a woman knitting during my speech was simply rude, but afterward she came up to ask some very cogent questions. When I pointed out the knitting, she said, "That's how I concentrate."

I once asked a man behind me who kept bumping me, "Are you blind?"

"Yes," he said, "as a matter of fact, I am!" and I turned to see him and a perturbed-looking, large guide dog.

Case Study

I was driving down the western, deserted part of the Massachusetts Turnpike when I saw in the distance a large dog stuck between the rails of the highway safety dividers on the roadside. I was driving a convertible with the top down and a manual transmission.

As I decelerated and pulled over to help the dog, it finally got free, and I found myself looking at a substantial black bear, three feet away, peering at me over the passenger door. I barely got the car into gear, my hand was shaking so much.

To paraphrase President Reagan, trust our perceptions, but then verify.

CHAPTER 9

Avoiding Brain Drain

Language in cultures and groups: The needs required to create not merely individual adeptness in these areas, but entire cultures of intelligent inquiry and profit, sharing language and listening that create dramatic organizational and market advantage.

Decreasing Inquiry Threat and Interrogations

Leadership success isn't about power or control or dominance. These misguided attributes are elements that can create an atmosphere of coercion and defensiveness. Leadership success is how you relate to others. It's your ability to create, build, and maintain communications and relationships that influence others to achieve the desired outcomes and results. Your content and your delivery must be conducive to creating this productive environment.

For every hagiography written about Steve Jobs or Donald Trump or Elon Musk or Tony Hsieh, there are tens of thousands of superb leaders using influence through intelligent language to maximize their organizations' productivity and profit.*

"It's not what you say, it's how you say it" is a common phrase that suggests that the words you use aren't as important as the *packaging or the delivery.* When it comes to effective communications and relationships, you need to be cognizant of what you are saying *and* how you are saying it (They go hand in hand, they are not mutually exclusive.) Your verbiage (the actual words you use) combined with your delivery will determine

---

* For example, as this is written, Tony Hsieh has instituted "Holacracy" (a leaderless ill-conceived nonmanagement system) at Zappos, which resulted in 200 immediate resignations and will probably no longer be used as intended by the time you read this.

whether your inquiry is perceived as an invitation to a conversation or as a threat or interrogation. Creating a *fight or flight* response in others creates an immediate brain drain for the topic at hand and diverts the intent and purpose of the conversation (unless, of course, your intent is to threaten or interrogate!).

Considerations and techniques for decreasing inquiry threat and interrogation are as follows:

- *The question "Why?"*: We have encouraged and guided you to proactively tell individuals and groups the *why* of any situation, regardless of whether they ask or not. However, when asking others *why*, you need to be cautious of how you frame your questions and the tone of voice you use. Asking why can put people on the defense. Your question, "Why did you do that?" can come across with a tone of voice that suggests, "What in the hell were you thinking???" There are a variety of neutral ways to ask "Why?" without ever using the word *why*, such as "What influenced your decision?" If you are on the receiving end of the *why* question, you can respond with some version of "Why do you ask?" *And:* "It would be helpful if I had a better understanding of what you're looking for." This positions the other person to frame why they are asking *why* before you respond, so you have a better understanding of purpose of the question asked of you. Of course, you need to respond in an "inquisitive and appropriate" manner with some relevance, that isn't defensive or challenging.
- *Accompany your inquiry with your reason for asking*: Don't expect others to know the reason(s) you are asking them questions. If they have to second-guess your intent, it creates an emotional distraction. Be forthcoming with the purpose of the inquiry to eliminate the perception of or the anticipation of threat.
- *Use rhetorical permission questions accompanied by a value statement*: Precede the inquiry by asking (not telling) if you can ask a few questions. And, include the reason or the value of the conversation. Example: "If I could ask you a few questions about the project, our discussion will help me

determine how we need to handle XYZ." Such preparatory questions (May I ask you...?) are, of course, rhetorical, so we call them *rhetorical permissions*.

- *Tone of voice, volume, inflection, rate of speech, facial expression, eye contact, body language*: Each of these verbal and nonverbal characteristics contribute to *how* you say things and how your audience interprets your inquiry. If you're spouting questions like an erupting Mount Vesuvius, others will believe they are in the midst of an interrogation (with a potential accusation soon to follow). On the other hand, if you're perceived as being aloof, unapproachable, and remote, it may interfere with others being responsive to you and engaged with you. It can create a tentativeness that is as detrimental as creating a defensive environment. Neither scenario is where you want to be.

To put a new twist on an old phrase, "It's what you ask (content), and how you ask it (context)."

Many years ago, a sociologist and psychologist by the name of Albert Mehrabian conducted some fascinating studies of people standing in lines and at social functions to see if they would allow someone in front of them or to be interrupted by others. He found that one's body language (e.g., a smile) raised the likelihood quite dramatically.

Unfortunately, many people have misinterpreted the study (especially professional speakers) to believe that most learning and rapport coming from speech is actually the nonverbal. This isn't remotely true. Words are the influencers, and nonverbal behavior is simply an augmentation when communicating.

Thus, when you are inquiring or questioning, it's important to keep your nonverbal behavior positive (e.g., don't *loom* over others), but it's absolutely vital to use the right language to find the information you seek.

Preventing the Response Stall

When you ask a question (or make a statement in a dialog), you expect a direct response. Sometimes you get one and sometimes you don't.

Sometimes you get a *response stall*. A stall can come in many forms, including a complete lack of any type of response at all. Here are a variety of stall techniques, some of which are short-term nuances and others are intentionally meant to stall next steps:

- No response at all (known as the stonewall)
- Repeating the very question you just asked in an inquisitive manner
- Responding with a question to your question
- Responding with a tangential or disparate comment (to which you would love to reply, "Interesting, but irrelevant.")
- Responding with an excuse, obstacle, or obscure reason as to why the process can't move forward (This is considered a stall objection or a smoke screen objection as we discussed in Chapter 6.)

In the case of what may appear to be a stall, you have no idea if:

- They didn't hear you (the words you said).
- They heard you (the words), but they didn't understand the questions or comment.
- They heard you, they understood you, and they either don't buy in or are put off by your question or comment and they are responding with a stall technique.

Note: The last situation above is the only actual stall as we're referencing it here. The other two situations warrant repeating or reframing. However, not getting past the first two situations (hearing and understanding) can create a legitimate impasse, not to mention significant confusion. You must determine which of the above is the case in order to know where to go next.

- If they didn't hear you, the solution is to restate the message.
- If they don't understand, you need to reframe the message; state the same meaning in another way.
- If they are objecting or stalling, deal with it.

The above may seem elementary, yet here's what can happen in the real world. If they don't understand or don't agree and instead you think they didn't hear you, you'll merely repeat your message louder and slower, which is guaranteed to come across as condescending or sarcastic. On the other hand, if they didn't hear or understand and you treat it as a stall, they're still a beat or two behind you and you're on the wrong track. In the moment, you need to be able to analyze and determine which situation you're dealing with.

When it comes to an actual response stall, ideally, you want to prevent it, which we addressed with the variety of techniques we've discussed in the previous eight chapters. Next best case is to overcome the stall (contingent action).

A stall can happen in any type of dialog, no matter how formal or informal in nature. The following situations are common examples of where, if you don't prevent it, you may need to *coach or prompt* someone through a response stall to keep the dialog moving forward.

- *Job Interview*: This dialog is the epitome of you asking a series of questions (or explaining expectations) while expecting the candidate to be forthcoming with information to determine if there's a match. If a candidate doesn't respond to any given question, it's up to you to *pull* the information from them. Which means, don't skip a question and move on just because the candidate is slow or reluctant to respond. Continue to probe. If the candidate says they haven't previously experienced what you're asking, try reframing the question in a way that they can relate to it. For example, if you're exploring leadership skills and success, they may not have been in a paid position with the title of leadership role, but they may have been in a nonpaid position that required particular leadership skills (volunteer role, association, board of directors, affiliates, and so on).

- *Tough buyer*: A stall is an extremely common objection in a traditional *seller–buyer* dialog regarding the purchase of products or services. It also applies when you are *selling* an idea or game plan internally or externally. The stall is a reason why they won't go forward at this time, but it is seldom the true objection. Stall objections can be variations on a theme of, "I need to talk with my business partner," "It's an interesting proposition, but now's not a good time for us," "We don't have the budget/resources/time allocated for this." If these are merely stall techniques (and not the true objection), attempting to overcome these is fruitless, as you're still left with the true objection. The technique to address this type of stall is to ultimately ask, "If it weren't for this situation (whatever they are citing), would you be willing to move forward on this?" Prior to the ultimate question, you may also be able to push through the stall with rhetorical questions or comments. For example, with the stall of "Now is not the right time," you might respond with, "If not now, when?" or "There's never a perfect time."

- *Reporter Questioning a Politician*: The politicians' stall is the *faux stall*. We've all seen it and heard it in action. The politician is asked a question and responds immediately without hesitation (and, at least, in their own minds, they respond very eloquently). However, they have not answered what was asked. The politician is either diverting the question they were asked or they are answering the question they want to be asked. They morph the conversation into their agenda, not the reporter's agenda and not the public's agenda. A savvy reporter will call them on it and restate the question. Even that doesn't mean the question will be answered as asked. One does not have to be a politician to mimic the *politician's faux stall*. Recognize it when it happens in response to your questions. Redirect to keep the focus on the point at hand.

A stall in aviation can be fatal. When a plane ascends too quickly at too sharp an angle, the appropriate lift beneath the wings diminishes and the nose of the plane drops. Unless the pilot recognizes the condition immediately and pulls the plane out of the stall by taking exactly the right steps at the right time, it's a guaranteed death spiral. Your role is to ask the right questions (or make the right statements) at the right time and ensure the responses are relevant in context, even if it means restating or reframing, in order to prevent or overcome the stall. Your role is to propel the formal and informal business conversations forward (lift and thrust in aviation) in order to move the business forward. Don't let unmanaged response stalls result in the inevitable crash and burn of that very progress.

Just as an airplane has a *stall speed* at which it is no longer able to keep itself in the air, we all have linguistic stall speeds at which point we're no longer able to keep a conversation alive or intent clear. This happens to the rich and the poor, the introvert and the extrovert, the celebrity and the *hoi polloi*:

- Remember when Katie Couric famously asked Sarah Palin during the election race what reading she did to acquire news and information? Nothing of any interest ensued, a complete stall. Yet, *anyone could have easily named The Wall Street Journal or The New York Times* if they wanted to fabricate believable sources. But Ms. Palin, astoundingly, couldn't even tell that white lie. (And she may well have been reading those newspapers.)
- The finalists in almost any beauty pageant face interview questions. The flubs, silences, and complete mishmash of facts are cannon fodder for hundreds of YouTube videos. Yet these are women accustomed to such questions from prior contests and preliminary qualifying. But they stall on a softball question such as "How should we combat world hunger?"*
- In political debates and press interviews, we observe politicians quite accustomed to this scrutiny fall apart. Bill Clinton actually managed to blurt out, "It depends what 'is' is." Various others have stared blankly when asked about foreign policy, the Federal Reserve, or the Constitution.

---

* I was a judge and coach of Miss America and Miss USA contests at the state level, and the women can easily learn how to handle most questions. They are very intelligent and very coachable.

- In your business, you've seen people at meetings, even
  prepared for a presentation, who look as though they want
  to dive under the table when asked a simple question such as
  "What are the risks involved?" or "Who else is doing this?"

You can prevent defaulting to a stall in your own responses by knowing your topic or discussion points very well. You should have examples and metaphors to back them up and give them relevancy.

You can prevent your own stall by knowing who else is present and what they are likely to ask or be most concerned about. President Obama, for a long time, was going to be asked about health care, no matter what. Are you going to be asked about sales, or product commercialization, or cash available, or absenteeism?

Profitable Language

To escape a stall, increase your air speed. That is, use some common sense to talk about the subject without worrying about what stalled you.

You can prevent the stall by controlling your nerves. *Choking* is not being able to do what you know needs to be done. *Panic* is forgetting what needs to be done. Stalls are caused by choking, when nervousness and stress confuse your rational responses (as in Sarah Palin's case). Be rested, be early, be prepared.

To mitigate the effects of a stall, learn this kind of profitable language:

- "I've just drawn the kind of blank where I forget my own
  name. Could you repeat that question?"
- "I don't want to risk a glib but incorrect response, can you
  give me some time to consider your point?"
- "Apologies, I was distracted, my fault. Can you say that
  again?"
- "Can we get back to that, there's something I need to ask you
  first?"

One of the causes of stalling—which can kill a sales call, job interview, or attempt at persuasion—is to fall prey to self-limiting beliefs.

Exterminating Self-Limiting Beliefs

Self-limiting beliefs become the bane of individuals and, collectively, their organizations. Their individual and cumulative nature makes an organization weak and vulnerable. They become the internal enemy of innovation and progress. They promote a synthetically heightened aversion to risk. Ultimately, self-limiting beliefs create a prevailing culture of self-fulfilling prophecies of what *can't* be accomplished or achieved, instead of what can be.

What are self-limiting beliefs? How do you recognize these undermining beliefs in yourself, in others, and within your culture? How do you exterminate them? And, how do you prevent new self-limiting beliefs from taking hold? Let's explore each of these.

What are self-limiting beliefs: Remember the phrase, "perception is reality?" What you perceive in your own observations becomes your own reality. Here's another facet of that concept, "Your beliefs are your reality." What you believe, especially about yourself, becomes your reality. Whether your beliefs are self-promoting or self-limiting, they are your truth. Your beliefs consciously and unconsciously inform and drive your behavior. For better or for worse, your beliefs about yourself are your truth and they become the motherboard of your personal operating system.

Self-limiting beliefs are self-imposed. They're not what others think about you (although, that may influence how you see yourself, if you allow it). Your self-limiting beliefs define who and what you are (or are not), in your own eyes. The negative aspects of self-limiting beliefs are focused on experiences from the past (recent or ancient history) and are carried into current times:

- Defining oneself by what one cannot do or be
- Comparisons and negative self-ratings of attributes and abilities
- Placing blame for circumstances that are *imposed*
- Being a *victim* of the environment
- Minimized self-worth and self esteem

How do you recognize self-limiting beliefs? There are patterns of thinking, communicating, and behavior that demonstrate the existence and manifestation of self-limiting beliefs.

Think about the times you've walked into a business meeting convinced that your proposal won't be accepted. Or getting into an athletic contest where you're sure you're outmatched by your counterparts. Or think of the times you were shocked that you prevailed, won, or succeeded.

You can recognize self-limiting beliefs by their manifestation of *certainty* of lack of success or surprise at actual success. You have mentally prepared for the negative, and if it's not fulfilled, then the positive astounds you.

Profitable Language

Your behaviors and reactions will tell you when and which self-limiting beliefs are operating. Change your internal language to reflect positive beliefs.

How do you exterminate self-limiting beliefs? If beliefs are reality, and those very beliefs are self-limiting, then it's your role to distort that reality, just as Steve Jobs did (as discussed in Chapter 7). Your mission is to create new, nonlimiting beliefs, which ultimately create a new reality. The limiting beliefs don't just magically go away. *They need to be replaced with a new way of thinking or believing.*

- Whether focusing on yourself or others, it's imperative that you recognize and capitalize on strengths. Too much time, effort, and angst is spent on weaknesses that are irrelevant to the circumstances. (The extreme of this is people who wear their weaknesses as a *badge of honor* as to why things can't happen.) The key is to maximize strengths and minimize weaknesses.
- Self-limiting beliefs can be a symptom of a fear of failure or of success. Counteracting the fear counteracts the self-limiting belief and vice versa.

  Find the cause of the fear, and then deal with it rationally:

  I fear public speaking.

  Cause: I'm afraid someone in the audience will make fun of me.

  Is that likely? Of course not, people want to see a success in terms on investing their time, and they'll want me to be successful and support me.

- Throw the baggage off the train. For years, counselors and therapists have advised clients that they need to drop the baggage they've been carrying to free themselves of the negative, nonproductive load they've been hauling around. If you're *on the train*, dropping the baggage merely releases the baggage from your grip. Interestingly enough, the baggage still shows up at your destination right beside you! So, the appropriate action is to *throw the baggage off the train* in order to truly leave it behind as you move forward.

How do you prevent new self-limiting beliefs from taking hold? Be conscious of how feedback influences your own self-talk, self-image, and confidence. Be selective in accepting and believing the feedback offered to you. Feedback is either solicited or unsolicited. Solicited feedback is sought and invited. It can be situational, meaning you request it for a specific event, occurrence, or behavior. Or you can give someone blanket permission to proactively provide feedback at any time. With solicited feedback, it's essential to engage people you trust to give you feedback.

Solicited feedback from those you trust is always in *your* own best interest. On the other hand, unsolicited feedback is imposed on you and is often someone else's agenda that is focused on you. Unsolicited feedback can be the sustenance and stimulant for self-limiting beliefs. Don't let that happen.

Building a Culture of Intelligent Inquiry

The Question is the Answer^{SM}. This is the foundation for building a culture of intelligent inquiry. Building this culture begins with you. It's your role to create, participate in, and model *intelligent inquiry* (versus creating a culture of inquiry that can span the spectrum from feeble questioning to an inquisition to an autocratic parental-type dominance). It's your role to be consistent in this approach in order to create a productive culture. (Remember, beliefs influence attitudes, which are manifest in behaviors. Instilling beliefs is what creates the culture.)

By definition, intelligent inquiry is an ongoing process that continually seeks an expansion of knowledge with an emphasis upon keeping an open mind concerning alternative theory. Sounds complicated? It's not. It's a matter of asking the right questions at the right time.

What beliefs, attitudes, and behaviors do you need to model and instill in order to create a culture of intelligent inquiry? The following are integral components:

- Inquiry is appropriate (and expected) at all levels of an organization. It's not merely a leader's or executive's *right*. It must be an equal opportunity regardless of position or title, without it being viewed as an inappropriate challenge of others.

- Avoid the intentional or unintentional belief that you expect a sycophantic culture. Lauding obsequious answers is counterproductive to a culture of inquiry.

- Encourage everyone in the organization to ask "Why?" so the value of processes or decisions never goes unspoken, or is not understood, or, worse yet, misunderstood.

- Think in reverse. When you want to tell, think in terms of *what is the unasked question* (yours or theirs) that prompts or generates the very response you are about to state. "Why is she asking that?" is an excellent internal question.

- In problem solving, encourage people to believe that it's effective and expected to ask questions to determine cause in order to prevent anyone from prematurely jumping to solutions. Managers are famous for the mantra, "If you're bringing me a problem, bring me a solution." The mantra needs to be, "If you're bringing me a problem, come to me with the possible and probable cause(s)." Instead of prematurely asking, "What do you think is the solution?" first ask "What do you think is the cause?" (Reminder, see Chapter 4, Critical Questioning Skills and Solving Problem, for the problem-solving process and related questions.)

- Be strategic in what you are asking and how to ask (versus asking haphazardly just for the sake of asking). Realize that questions can be focused on the past, present, or future. They can be focused on fact, opinion, or speculation.

- The Socratic method in its purest form is asking exploratory questions in which there may not be one right answer. It's meant to stimulate discussion and debate. That very method has morphed into a teaching method where the *instructor* asks questions in order for the audience to experience and learn. It's meant to promote logic and critical thinking. If you only ask questions in which there is a right answer, you may be creating an effective learning environment. However, be aware, you cannot create a culture of intelligent inquiry solely via this method. You run the risk of being perceived as merely *testing people* to determine if they know the right answer. The Socratic inquiry is merely one tool in creating a culture of intelligent inquiry, not the only tool.
- Asking the right question at the right time creates an environment of engagement. Questions create active participation. Consistently telling or directing, with the absence of questions, is a passive environment.

How do you know when this very culture you are creating and instilling is *actually taking hold?*

Here are some hallmarks of a culture of intelligent inquiry:

- People don't *jump to cause.* They don't say, "This is another instance of …" but rather immediately seek to find answers, *not blame.*
- Validation and verification are naturally sought. "Here's the issue, here are optional effective responses, and here's how I know this."
- Due diligence is performed on new initiatives and projects, as if the organization were buying or acquiring or merging. Due diligence becomes a process, not an erratic undertaking.
- Feedback, alternative views, and healthy debate are encouraged. No one believes that *self-editing* is required before voicing an opinion.
- The organization's self-interest is represented in the opinions and ideas expressed. Fiefdoms and silos are disassembled and

there is no more fertile ground for them. All top executives see themselves as functional heads (e.g., sales or R&D) but *also as corporate officers.*

Inquiry, in and of itself, can be unproductively undermining or it can be productively healthy. Intelligent inquiry is with the intent of being productive and positive for *all involved.* Even when it seems to be challenging or uncomfortable (for you and for the audience), it should always be productively healthy. The following are additional tips in creating a healthy culture of intelligent inquiry:

- Don't always take responses at face value as to what you think the other person may say or what they may mean. It's effective to continue to probe (drill down) by asking additional clarifying questions such as:

  Tell me more …
  What brings you to that conclusion?
  If that weren't a factor, what would happen?
  What would cause this to fail?
  What are the exceptions to this situation?
  What if …?
  How will we know if … ?
  How could we … ?

Inquiry is one aspect of success. At some point, inquiry must lead to a conclusion, a decision, an action. But you'll find that it does so more efficaciously than not utilizing it and produces greater harmony and consensus, which are important by-products.

Building a culture of intelligent inquiry is one element of exercising and promoting productivity in an organization. It's not productivity in terms of the cliché *harder, faster, more.* It's a type of productivity that's not easily quantifiable on its own, and yet it propels individuals and organizations to success in a variety of ways. A culture of intelligent inquiry is the antithesis of individual and collective brain drain.

Profitable Language

"Leadership is in the hands of the person who asks the next GREAT question." Anonymous.

"Leadership is in the hands of the person who creates a culture of intelligent inquiry." Wilkerson and Weiss.

CHAPTER 10

The Language of the Future

What language is constant and what is merely trend? This is the "action planning" stage where we help you through the steps to make the approaches highly personal, immediately gratifying, and a part of the nature of your work and fabric of your spoken and written business and life.

What Is Really "Future Tense"?

Experts make predictions. They aren't always right, but true experts are right more often than they're wrong.

If we include in the boat of *expertise* authority, moral suasion, influence, respect, and admiration as shipmates, then we can conclude that in your personal life and your business pursuits your expertise is vital. You want colleagues to respect you. You'd no doubt prefer that your family loved and admired you. You'd even want adversaries to hold you in respect and esteem, not see you as a *pushover*, but rather as a worthy opponent.

We've tried to show, if nothing else, that language is the underpinning of all your transactions. Therefore, your vocabulary and phrasing, your metaphors and examples, your tone and inflection will determine your success and expertise.

Profitable Language

Expertise is never claimed but rather bestowed.

Language is fungible. There are considerable debates about whether we should hold a *purist* position and defend the proper usage down to the last participle and gerund or whether language evolved with society and we should consider modern colloquialism as the norm without being dissed. (Note that our spell checker did not question *dissed*.)

Here are some guidelines to maintaining the proper *future tense* in your approach to language:

1. Be aware of environment. Colloquial speech probably doesn't belong at a Unilever board meeting, but is quite common at Apple management sessions. What is culturally appropriate?

2. Be aware of context. The nature of the issue and its severity or lack of severity will probably influence your choices. For example, you might say to someone giving a motivational speech to a team, "You crushed that!" But I wouldn't compliment the person giving a eulogy at a funeral with that same phrase.

3. Consider your position. You're of a certain age, in a certain business or professional station in life, you're married or unmarried, leader or follower. At my age I find it important to understand what teenagers are talking about, but not to try to talk like them even when talking to them. It's sort of like the fact that I can understand Spanish better than speak it. I can tell that you've asked me to step into the next room, but if I ask you for directions, I might find myself directed into the alley.

4. Understand that meanings change. The word *gay* for example has changed in its primary denotation considerably. Some words are purely *scientific* in their clear intent—a tree is a tree (apologies to Joyce Kilmer). But *joint, grass,* and *weed* can have a more *magical* connotation.

5. Be sensitive to regional differences. A *hoagie, sub,* and *grinder* are all similar sandwiches, but some are unknown in certain parts of the country. Some regions say *soda,* others *pop.* In some parts of Asia, *all* of what we'd call *soda* is requested by asking for *Coke* (which itself has a magical meaning, as well).

6. Test out trends. Not all new locutions are permanent. Some are no more than advertising failed attempts to gain notice. Others are highly regionalized. Be careful that you don't become less understood by using strange constructions. (I've never understood *went extinct* or *went missing.*) The sartorial equivalent is found in men who wear their baseball hats backward with the visor in the rear and then have to shield their eyes from the sun.

While there will be struggles to turn *between you and I* into acceptable speech, the immutable fact is that the *future tense* is about clarity. The litmus test for successful language will be quite simple:

- Do they understand me accurately?
- Are they doing what I ask?
- Am I being as succinct as possible?

There's not much more to desire! Bear in mind that the Gettysburg Address was written on the back of an envelope and required barely more than two minutes to deliver in its entirety. It remains one of the most moving and profound pieces ever written about sacrifice and freedom. Verbosity does not connote expertise. Terseness does.

People are adults. They are fully able to ask questions if they don't understand you (and provided you believe in a culture of intelligent inquiry). Thus, *tell people what they need to know, not everything that you know.* My tree expert insists on telling me the history of elms or the nature of the development of caterpillars chomping on the leaves. I just want the trees protected. My air conditioning guy keeps explaining about BTUs and thermal inversions and temperature deltas.

I just want the rooms cooled.

The ability to engage in *future tense* will depend upon two factors: Your grounding and confidence in your language, and your adaptations to the conditions mentioned earlier.

But there is another rather major element.

Electronic Language

Walt Mossberg is the former technology columnist for *The Wall Street Journal*. He and I were talking one day on the way to an event when he said,

> I don't know why people say, "I'll go on the internet for that," because they don't seem to realize that they are *always* on the internet. It's as silly as saying, when you want to toast some bread, 'I think I'll go on the electric grid.' We need to stop making that distinction.

Our language of the future will increasingly be by electronic means. That includes social media, YouTube, business media, Skype, GoTo-Meeting, and any number of developing technologies that accommodate print, audio, and video. Many meetings are now streaming, we tend to post on Facebook more than we would ever write conventional letters, and we tend to text a shorthand of the language even more often than that.

What does this mean for language use?

- We need to separate out the informal uses appropriate for technology from the more formal uses appropriate for relationships. For example, I saw a speaker at a business meeting who wanted to convey emphasis on growth use this construction: "We want to achieve hashtag growth." This was meant to limn the Twitter device for creating common themes and threads, but it failed orally and the accompanying hand signals for *hashtag* just made it worse.
- We have to focus on being succinct more than ever. It's far easier to become bored over remote communication than in person. I fell asleep once during a mentoring call by phone where the other person was droning on with background about some incident where help was needed. And we have all seen people doze off even in meetings in real time. Electronic speech relies far more on quick hits, and frequent to and fro. Think of the fast reflexes of ping pong, not the boring baseline volleys in tennis.
- Language is far less reinforced by nonverbal behavior. Even when we're using video, not only do we see a more limited view of the other person's body language, but we tend to be far less effusive with our body language. You can't stand up, or roam away from the camera, or really do much outside of the frame. There is far less nonverbal power, meaning your speech has to have still more power.
- Group interaction is more severely limited. Despite constant advances in technology, those who are boldest, or loudest,

or hold the most senior positions will tend to dominate in conversations and interactions of more than two people. That will require either a formal agenda allocating *air time* to everyone or, more likely, a far more assertive type of behavior to convey your point and respond to those of others.

- Differing time frames will impact energy and alertness. I run global groups that often prefer to meet in real time and not listen to recordings. Even choosing a time that's least disruptive, there are people on the phone at 4 in the morning or midnight. Our biorhythms aren't meant for that kind of disruption and we have to pay even more attention to our language in view of fatigue.

- Finally, the technology that allows for instantaneous and global communication at any time also creates a subtle language issue. Although the world language is *de facto* English (formally, in air traffic control, for example, and informally in that some companies in Germany demand that English be used internally), it is not always *the same English*. Increasingly, we are interacting with people who don't understand our sports metaphor (what we call soccer, they call football), or political reference, or jargon, or cultural connotation. We have to be careful to use clear language and not *merely* English. A classic failure here was the outsourced call centers to India, filled with American kitsch, and with everyone wearing American baseball caps, but which failed dismally to relate to American callers. Most have been returned to the United States despite higher labor costs because of the costs of customer complaints.

While there is no *electronic language*, there are constraints placed on language by electronics. It's important to consider these and take proper preventive actions.

Remember, even after all this time, no one has ever figured out how to stop an e-mail once you hit *send*, and we've all hit *send* and regretted it a nanosecond later.

The Value of Silence

Our book has been about language, which requires, well, sound. But often, language becomes more powerful in the presence of silence.

What you don't say can be far more powerful than what you do say in many instances. Emerson said, "What you are speaks so loudly I can't hear what you say." A colleague of ours, Steven Gaffney, is an expert in honest communications. One of his most salient points is that what's unsaid can be more important than what is said.

All of us have been in the position where, threatened by a three-second silence that seemed like 20 minutes, we said something utterly banal and insipid, thereby undermining our cause and diminishing our presence. We often do this with a superior or someone we are trying to impress—a job interview, a meeting at work, a legal proceeding. Lawyers abjure a verbose or overly volunteering witness on their behalf. They tell us to solely answer what we're asked, nothing more. Never volunteer anything that you haven't been asked. (And, commensurately, they are taught never to ask a question for which they do not already know the answer.)

A silence is often a bargaining chip, and countering it is often a concession. Listen to poor speakers. They fill every void with *er*, or *ah*, or *you know*, or *okay*, or they laugh for no reason. They fear the silence and consequently make nothing more than distracting noises. As a speech coach with many clients, I play back tapes of their talks and they are astounded at the inarticulate sounds they never realized they were uttering.

The best poker players don't talk, except to indicate their bets. Silence is by far the preferred ambiance for prayer or meditation or contemplation. Most of us can perhaps recall the great Simon and Garfunkel song, "The Sounds of Silence."*

Why should we mix in a healthy dose of silence to aid and abet the effectiveness of our language?

1. It's an excellent negotiating tactic. It's one thing to scream at a realtor, "We *love* this house," and pay full asking price, but it's another to simply stay quiet as the realtor explains the positives, conveniently

---

* Paul Simon music and lyrics, Columbia Records, 1964.

overlooks the negatives, and wonders what on earth you're thinking and whether a 15-percent price drop might sway you.

2. You can elicit responses from others more easily on many occasions—more easily than trying to convince them with logic. Others will tend to *step into* the silence, and if you're patient, you might just learn something of immense value. Police have been known just to let suspects sit with them after asking a question, as the interviewee begins to offer more and more detail as the silence threatens them. ("Maybe I was on 14th St. at that time, and maybe I did happen to pass her in the dark ...")

3. You force the succinctness on yourself that we discussed earlier. If you can create, sustain, and tolerate silence, then by definition you have probably told people what they need to know, not everything you know, and you can simply await their next questions or comments. The more silence, the less you're talking; the less you're talking, the more you have to make your points in tight language and time frames.

4. You give yourself time to think. It's tough to think while you're rattling on and tough to think while you're trying to track someone else rattling on. But with even 10 seconds of silence, you can reorder your thoughts, create an example, suggest a course of action, and so forth.

5. You seem far more deliberate and wise. I've always been somewhat disenchanted by the people (especially, for some reason, my college professors) who immediately ran on with an answer to a question just asked. While it could be that they hear the question often, it could also be that we're hearing a *stock* answer not really pertinent to our condition. Lawyers and doctors worry me greatly when they respond hastily because I don't think they're listening, but rather labeling me and providing *response 6.3*. That can have dire implications for one's legal and physical health. But I always admired the professor who took a puff on a pipe (when that was allowed) or the speaker who pauses and considers the inquiry—allowing everyone to wait in eager, anticipatory silence—while formulating an answer.

We live in an age and are entering a future in which stimuli will continue to multiply. While I'm writing this, I've heard three beeps on my phone, which I forgot to turn off, indicating incoming messages. Our future will be clogged with noise from friends, family, advertisers, news, recreation, entertainment, mobile access, and so forth.

We need to create some silence.

Don't become so enamored with language that you shun silence. You're not getting paid by the word, nor are you respected by the amount of air time you use.

Many years ago, in the classic TV show "Get Smart," I believe they had a *cone of silence*. They bought it at discount on the show, so it never worked correctly for the spies in the series. But you can create your own *cone of silence* if you take pains to allow yourself the option and the luxury.

Therapists bask in silence, waiting, often out of direct sight, for the patient to say something, allowing the patient to take the next step, establish the next direction.

I've often sat silent for 30 minutes or so listening to a group talk over each other trying to sort out an issue, then rise and go to the board to show them what I heard and figured out while I sat there in my own *cone of silence*.

It all depends on what you're telling yourself.

Self-Language

The final message of our book is about the language you speak, but to yourself. The ancient philosophical debate is about whether thought or words came first, a sort of cognitive *chicken or egg*. Yet, how do you think if you have no means—no tools—to express your thoughts?

Over the past decade or more, *positive psychology* has become a major field of study and a vital source of self-development. Popularized by impressive academicians, such as Dr. Martin Seligman at the University of Pennsylvania,* the basic tenet is that the *self-talk* one uses influences behavior profoundly.

---

* See, for example, https://www.authentichappiness.sas.upenn.edu

Dr. Dan Gilbert, at Harvard,* has investigated *synthetic happiness*, showing that what we once thought was pure rationalization (e.g., that accident taught me an important lesson; getting fired was the best thing that ever happened to me) is actually a highly effective way of talking to ourselves to create happiness. People who do so on a regular basis he found to be far happier than those who solely relied on *traditional* events such as birthdays, anniversaries, births, and so forth.

In other words, scientists are more convinced than ever by empirical evidence and research that the language we use with ourselves has the most extensive and dramatic impact on our success in life—or lack of it.

What is the language you use about yourself? Have you bothered to examine it? Other people (short of therapeutic intervention) can't do that for you, and you're not really paying attention most of the time, any more than you're conscious of your constant, small adjustments with the steering wheel as you drive the car.

You need to step back from that *unconscious competency* to *conscious competency* in order to examine what you do without thinking about it.

Unconscious competency

Conscious competency

Conscious incompetency

Unconscious incompetency

As you can see in the progression above, there are things we don't do well without realizing it, which is why some people's attire or singing immediately draws groans from most others. Then there are things that we're intensely aware we don't do well—playing a piano would be one of mine or dancing a tango another.

There are things we do well by focusing on them, such as writing this book or hitting a golf ball. And, then, there are things we do well without thinking, such as making the knot in a tie or giving an extemporaneous talk.

In order to study your self-language, you must step into conscious competency and ask what, precisely, you say to yourself. Some examples:

---

* http://www.danielgilbert.com.

- When you succeed, do you say you're talented and worked hard, or you were lucky?
- When you fail, do you say you learned something for next time or that you have no talent?
- When you trip over a piece of furniture, do you say that someone put it in an inappropriate place or do you remind yourself that you're clumsy?
- Do you generalize specific positives into a generalization or specific negatives into a generalization (I convinced them, I'm excellent at persuasion, or I didn't convince them, I have lousy interpersonal skills)?

I tell salespeople I coach all the time that a rejection by a prospect is not a reflection on one's sales skills, but merely the fact that that person, at that time, did not purchase what you were selling. That could be different tomorrow, with another person or the same person. (Which is why sales persistence is such an asset, not sales surrender when you hear a *no*.)

Your self-language is an ongoing narrative, the novel of your life that you write every day. The question that only you can answer is: Will every day be the same or be an improvement? That will depend on how you talk to yourself.

Yogi Berra, the surprisingly insightful observer of human behavior, observed that "Baseball is 90 percent mental, and the other half physical." You can watch golfers' success by what they tell themselves they can do or can't do on the course. Lesser talented athletes in all sports beat superior competition all the time because they are more mentally prepared. Sports "motivational coaches" proliferate.

It has become incredibly clear that *the most* important language you ever use is also the language you use most constantly—with yourself. As we come to the conclusion of this book, we want to urge you to apply the skills and ideas consistently to this area. Specifically:

- Pause before major decisions, events, and activities and ask yourself what kind of language you're using to describe it and your participation and chances for success.

- Treat negative events (financial setback, lost promotion, relationship ending) as isolated incidents that have no bearing on tomorrow, and positive events (financial gain, promotion obtained, new relationship) as examples of generalized strengths (investment acumen, talents, attraction).
- Deliberately talk to yourself briefly first thing in the morning and just before going to bed. Take 30 seconds to remind yourself of what you've done well and why and what you intend to do well and why. Firmly secure these consciously so that they can become part of your unconscious competency.
- Review your day and determine what you were saying to yourself prior to major events and how that contributed to your success or setback. Remind yourself of what you need to abandon or repeat in the future.

The language of success is a combination of a common use of the powerful techniques we've presented *combined with* your own ability and inclination to use them with discipline and frequency. Every business today is in the communications business, and that will continue tomorrow.

And every person's success in business—and in life—is a matter of the language they use.

Profitable Language

What are you saying to yourself right now, and does it need to change or be reinforced?

Index

OTHER TITLES IN OUR CORPORATE COMMUNICATION COLLECTION

Debbie DuFrene, Stephen F. Austin State University, Editor

- *Managerial Communication: Evaluating the Right Dose* by J. David Johnson
- *Web Content: A Writer's Guide* by Janet Mizrahi
- *Intercultural Communication for Managers* by Michael B. Goodman
- *Persuasive Business Presentations: Using the Problem-Solution Method to Influence Decision Makers to Take Action* by Gary May
- *SPeak Performance: Using the Power of Metaphors to Communicate Vision, Motivate People, and Lead Your Organization to Success* by Jim Walz
- *Today's Business Communication: A How-To Guide for the Modern Professional* by Jason L. Snyder and Robert Forbus
- *Leadership Talk: A Discourse Approach to Leader Emergence* by Robyn Walker and Jolanta Aritz
- *Communication Beyond Boundaries* by Payal Mehra
- *Managerial Communication* by Reginald L. Bell and Jeanette S. Martin
- *Writing for the Workplace: Business Communication for Professionals* by Janet Mizrahi
- *Get Along, Get It Done, Get Ahead: Interpersonal Communication in the Diverse Workplace* by Geraldine E. Hynes

Announcing the Business Expert Press Digital Library

Concise e-books business students need for classroom and research

This book can also be purchased in an e-book collection by your library as

- a one-time purchase,
- that is owned forever,
- allows for simultaneous readers,
- has no restrictions on printing, and
- can be downloaded as PDFs from within the library community.

Our digital library collections are a great solution to beat the rising cost of textbooks. E-books can be loaded into their course management systems or onto students' e-book readers.
The **Business Expert Press** digital libraries are very affordable, with no obligation to buy in future years. For more information, please visit **www.businessexpertpress.com/librarians**. To set up a trial in the United States, please email **sales@businessexpertpress.com**.